The Joy
of Selling

When a man has once broken through the paper walls of everyday circumstance, those insubstantial walls that hold so many of us securely prisoned from the cradle to the grave, he has made a discovery. If the world does not please you, *you can change it.* Determine to alter it at any price, and you can change it altogether. You may change it to something sinister and angry, to something appalling, but it may be you will change it to something brighter, something more agreeable, and at the worst something much more interesting. There is only one sort of man who is absolutely to blame for his own misery, and that is the man who finds life dull and dreary.

H. G. WELLS

The Joy of Selling

MICHAEL BEER

MERCURY BOOKS
Published by W.H. Allen & Co. Plc

First published in 1988
by the Mercury Books Division of
W.H. Allen & Co. Plc
44 Hill Street, London W1X 8LB

Set in Concorde by Phoenix Photosetting,
Printed and bound in Great Britain by
Mackays of Chatham PLC, Chatham, Kent

British Library Cataloguing in Publication Data

Beer, Michael, *1926–*
    The joy of selling.
    1. Salesmanship
    I. Title
    685.8'5

ISBN 1–85252–024–8

Contents

PART 1

Getting into the
wonderful world of selling

1

Who are you?

I'm Michael Beer and I'm a salesman. If you stay with me I shall change your attitude towards the world of selling. And if you allow me, I'll change your life in a way that you may not think possible.

You know my name and I don't know yours, but I do know something about you. (Actually I know two things about you – tell you about the second one in a moment.) I know that you are not getting much joy from your present job. I know this because if you were you wouldn't have bothered to pick up this book.

You are an estimator, a teacher, a welder, a branch manager or the cashier at a fast-food emporium. You get up every morning at the same time, take a bus or train or car into work where you do pretty well the same thing every day. You work with people you don't particularly like, you do things which don't excite you. At the end of the week or month you get a pay packet or cheque which doesn't send you into transports of ecstasy. You get a couple of weeks' leave every year which pass in a flash. When you come back to the same old job the year stretches out in front of you, a featureless wasteland of boredom, petty irritations and frustrations.

Or, you may be a salesman already. In that case you picked up this book with a cynical and sceptical grimace, to flip through the pages and find out just how the author is planning to rip off the unsuspecting suckers simple enough to buy the book. You *know* that the title of the book is a lot of hooey – there *is* no joy in selling, and you prove it every day of your life. If there was any way you could get out of the selling business you'd do it like a shot. So who is this Beer who thinks he can fool you into believing that there's joy in the peddling game?

For you, my salesman friend, the message is clear and simple: there *is* joy in selling. If you aren't getting any it only means that you are in the wrong sort of selling – wrong for you, that is – or you are going about it in the wrong way. Now that may sound blunt and even offensive, but I'm not here to make happy noises at you. I intend to change your life. Selling is not merely another way of making a living; it is a whole wonderful world, and you can prove it. Ask a successful salesman if he would change his job and you will get any number of reactions, depending on the personality of the salesman. He will either judge you crazy, throw you out of the room, or laugh himself silly. Whatever he does, you will be in no doubt that he would no more change his job than he would cut his throat.

Oh, sure, you say. The really successful salesman has the world by the short hair on a downhill pull. He earns plenty, he generally picks his own times to work, he has the respect of his colleagues and bosses – he lives the life of Riley. But the crackerjack salesman is practically an endangered species: there are very, very few of them. And the reason is that in order to be in that league you have to have some very special characteristics. You have to have the gift of the gab, you have to be able to talk a dog down off a butcher's wagon, you need the hide of a rhinoceros, and the ability to high-pressure your poor listener until he doesn't know which way is South – there aren't many of those characters around.

Now, that is a lot of bull.

I don't know who first started this story that good salesmen are made in a special mould which they break at birth. That only a certain type of person can do well in selling – and in any case to do well you have to bulldoze, badger and bullyrag your customers. Much better to stay in your job as trainee in the Stock Department, and if you really do well this year and pull out all the stops maybe they will let you move your desk away from the tea table.

I'm not sneering at a man who, while he has been attracted to the idea of selling as a career, has been put off by the horror stories from friends and family. For most of you selling would mean giving up a secure job. While it might not be the most exciting thing in your life it does at least give you a living income and a chance to climb, however slowly, the ladder to higher things. To turn your back on this and embark on a sea which looks very much wider and rougher than anything you have experienced takes courage. You may already be locked into a certain minimum standard of living, with a mortgage and all the other expenses which must be paid at the end of the week or month. Dare you let go of the substance to grasp at the shadow?

I have written this book for the person who has at one time or another thought: 'Why shouldn't I be able to sell?' but who has gone no further. There was nobody to tell him how to get into the business of selling, what to sell, who to work for, how he wants to be paid for what he does, and all the other vital questions which jump into the mind whenever a completely new venture is envisaged. If you are such a person, or if you are already in selling but are getting no joy (either emotional or financial) from it, then what follows in these pages was tailor-made for you. It is a distillation of my lifetime in selling, in managing salesmen, and in training salesmen and sales managers.

There is no fiction in this book; every word is true. I have not tried to gloss over the problems of a career in selling, I have nowhere said that selling is something you can do on a rainy Saturday afternoon from an easy chair while watching reruns of *Little House on the Prairie*. If you decide to go for selling as a way of life you are going to have to do it with all your heart, or give up the idea right now. Anything worthwhile, from running a ten-second hundred yards to winning the blue ribbon at the chrysanthemum show, requires perspiration and dedication, and selling is no exception.

You know this already, of course. What is worrying you at the moment is the uncertainty: 'Could I make a success of selling? I have no special skills, I don't have a glib tongue, I'm not a specially attractive personality and I don't even particularly like meeting people. Everything I have ever heard about successful salespeople seems to indicate that they have the things that I don't have. In addition to all that, the idea of buttonholing someone and trying to take money from him in exchange for a product which he has never heard of, does not want or need and cannot afford anyway – that petrifies me. Be honest, now; admit that not everybody can sell, and with my list of shortcomings I must be one of those who can't.'

Well, *can* John or Janet Average find fame, riches – and joy – in the selling business? That's what we have to find out.

Before we do, please notice that I am talking about Janet as well as John. The linguistics experts haven't yet come up with a satisfactory pronoun which includes both masculine and feminine, and since it is clumsy to keep writing 'he and/or she' I have had to use the usual 'he' when I talk of a salesman (which is also, of course, a restricted way of talking about someone who makes a living by selling). None of this means, however, that we are talking only about men. Let's be very certain of this: there isn't a single thing in this entire book which applies only to men. There isn't a single thing here which women can't do just as well as men. We might as well get that behind us before we start, although we shall go into it a little more fully in the next chapter.

All right – can you sell? Male or female, young or old, new at the game or an old hand – could you cut it in selling?

Come with me and find out.

2

> ## *'Who, me? I couldn't sell lifebelts on the Titanic!'*

Can you sell successfully?

Let's take an analogy. Could a good music teacher turn me into a concert pianist? No, he could not. I cannot read a note of music, I have never played the piano, and I am long past the age when aspiring concert pianists start learning. But suppose I wanted to play the piano competently; not merely bash out *Humoresque* very badly, but play with confidence, authority and even flair. Suppose that I still possess all ten fingers, none of them afflicted with the agonies of arthritis; suppose that I was able to set aside adequate time each day; suppose I had the services of a good teacher; suppose that I was determined to succeed in this new venture.

Suppose all this. Would you say that at the end of, say, a year of dedicated learning and practising, I could sit down at the piano and give a successful and competent recital? Of course I could.

Now, mind, I didn't say that my performance would fill the London Palladium with enthusiastic fans. We are not talking international virtuoso here. We are saying that granted the conditions, any average person could produce results which would be perfectly competent. Not inspired, but *competent*. The dictionary defines that word as: 'Having sufficient skill; suitable or adequate for the purpose'. That's it. I would have succeeded in what I set out to do.

Can you sell successfully? Can this book turn you into a crackerjack salesman, one of those who could sell earthquake insurance to an Eskimo? Yes and no. Yes, you can sell successfully, and no, it won't make you an ace salesman.

Right here is where this book differs from every other book,

[13]

film, tape or course on selling. They all claim that after being exposed to their special teaching you will ride out on a blazing saddle and sell up a storm. I don't say that. I don't guarantee to turn you into a Rubinstein or an Ashkenazy. What I will do if you stay with me all the way is show you how to decide what to sell, how to get into selling, and how to produce a simple and effective presentation. If you work at it, this will give you the results, the orders, the sales volume, the satisfaction and joy – not to speak of money – which you deserve in your job.

But hang on there, Beer. Who are you to say that I *can't* be one of the elite, the really top salespeople? Well, I don't say you can't; all I say is that I can't make you one, and nor can anyone else. Bjorn Borg had the advantage of the best of trainers, but no coach made Borg the most successful tennis player of all time – he did that himself. After all the techniques have been mastered, after bodily perfection has been reached, what puts a person into that triple-A bracket right at the top is what goes on in his head. Lord Thomson of Fleet said: 'The recipe for success? Simple; an overwhelming desire to succeed.' Borg had it, and it took him to the top – and when he lost it he had the courage and good sense to quit.

So. I said that without ever meeting you I knew two things about you. One was that you were not getting much joy from your job. The other is that you can sell. Now, that's about as dogmatic and categorical a statement as it's possible to make, and while it is true, it's just a little sneaky, because there is a condition attached to it. Oh, you can sell successfully, all right, and I promise to show you how; I'll stay with you every step of the way. But you have to bring this one thing along with you. It is all I ask of you, but it is an absolutely essential condition of your success. It is so important that it deserves a line to itself:

You have to *want* it.

That's it; that's all there is. You have to want to sell. You must want to be able to say: 'I really helped those people! They are going to be doing something a little better tomorrow than they were doing today. Why? Because of what I told them!'

When a salesman first realises that he has *changed the thinking of someone else* it is as though a light has come on inside him. Changed his thinking, mind you, not through a high-pressure 'spiel', not through artificial enthusiasm or waving his arms around or banging on the desk, but through a simple, logical and convincing presentation. When a salesman does this it changes his whole attitude towards his job. If you have never had anyone say to you: 'I want to thank you for suggesting that product to me. It has made a tremendous difference; I'm glad I took your advice', then you have missed one of the great satisfactions of life. When someone calls you and says: 'You did a good job for us last time so I'm calling to ask for your help again' you begin to wonder why you didn't get into this wonderful world of selling years ago.

Yes, but it isn't always like that, is it, Beer? Customers praising you, asking your advice, deferring to your opinion – that's cloud-cuckoo-land, right?

Right. Selling is not all blue skies and roses all the way. What is the world of selling *really* like?

Let's see.

3

The worst job in the world
– the best job in the world

Selling is the worst job in the world if you are no good at it. Think about it. The unsuccessful salesman drags himself out of bed every morning to face a day in which he already knows he will be confronted by people who will:

- Keep him waiting because 'It's only a salesman, sir.'
- Talk down at him as though he were the lowest form of life.
- Accuse him of high-pressure tactics.
- Interrupt his sales presentation.
- Call him a liar.
- Throw him out (sometimes physically).

When he gets home after a day like this he is likely to be met by a wife who tells him that her brother has just had another promotion and salary increase (he has a *respectable* job, see). And since the washing machine has now broken down for the third time can they afford to buy a new one? (They can't.)

In addition he is in constant contact with people like his father-in-law who wonders audibly what possessed his daughter to marry a bloody pedlar. By friends who ask him whether he is still a salesman after all these years. Has he not thought of changing his job to something with more of a future?

At work, things are no better. His sales manager is continually calling for more sales volume. No matter how hard he tries or how many hours he puts in, he gets much nagging and very little credit. His colleagues give him little sympathy. They have problems of their own and in any case they are to a large extent in opposition to him, since everything is relative, and the better he is the worse they look, and vice versa. The other divisions of the company, from Finance to Production, treat him as an overpaid and underworked nuisance. He knows perfectly well that if a slot ever opened up in Management he would be the last to be considered for it. His past is an embarrassment of humiliations at the hands of cold-eyed receptionists, hard-nosed assistant buyers and hostile telephonists. His present is a dreary and unproductive grind. His future is a grey blur.

One thing about selling which makes it such an awful way of making a living is that your failures can't be hidden as they can in many other jobs. You can be a not-very-good accounting clerk, a mediocre office supervisor or a below-average storeman, and your inadequacies can be hidden for years. But a salesman is judged first and foremost by his sales figures, and when the computer spits them out at the end of the month they are out there on display for all the world to see.

The unsuccessful salesman hates sales contests and incentive schemes because when the results are read out at the prize-giving his name comes just before the coffee-break announcement. He sidles into the sales office with his eyes averted from the huge chart on the wall which shows in full colour the sales-against-quota figures for all the sales team. It always gives him stomach-cramps to look at it.

He has never had a new company car; he gets the one passed down by the top salesman. If he is late for a sales meeting they start without him and he gets hell; they *wait* for the good salesmen.

At the office party he gets placed at the bottom of the table and the marketing director can't remember his name. He gets condescension from the order clerks and pity from the girls in the Stats department. He would gladly change his job, but with the lousy references he would get from his company, who would hire him?

In truth, selling is the worst job in the world – if you are no good at it.

I have painted this picture in blood and gore so that you may be in no doubt about what it means to be an unsuccessful salesman.

I don't want anyone calling me and cursing the day he picked up this book and was persuaded to give up a good job to endure a lifetime of regret. I concede that I have lumped all the nasties together to make the picture as black as possible, and that for most unsuccessful salesmen the situation is not as horrific as this. For most of them the daily round is not very good, not very bad – just very medium. They don't have all that many catastrophes but they certainly don't have triumphs, and they sure as nuts are not getting any *joy*, and that is what it is all about.

Ah, but turn it over and look at the other side. Selling is the best job in the world – if you are good at it. Selling is unique in this respect, that *if* you are good at it then you *must* be enjoying it. This is by no means true of any other way of making a living. Read that last sentence over again; it is a vitally important point to bear in mind when you are considering a change of direction in your career.

Right at this moment I can think of three people who are good at their jobs. In fact, they are very good indeed, they are highly respected in their fields; yet they get no joy from what they do. They are a doctor, the technical manager of a contracting company, and a financial director. Oh, there may be a temporary satisfaction in overcoming a sticky problem from time to time, but joy? No way. The technical manager told me as he prepared to go back to work after his vacation: 'I'm not looking forward to another year of calculating how much gravel a front-end loader can shift.' The doctor once said that ninety-nine per cent of his patients bring in complaints which are so mundane and routine that he diagnoses and treats them with his mind on something else. The financial director is on the board of a large company, a leader in its field, and his division works with the precision of a chronometer. Yet he goes through life with the disgruntled air of someone who has been cheated out of something which he can't quite put his finger on.

All of them, you see, successful men, measured by any of the standards we normally apply. Successful? Yes. Happy in their work? *Joyful?* No.

But take the successful salesman. Talk to him about his job. Watch his eyes light up. Listen to the warmth in his voice. Feel the enthusiasm as he talks about the tough ones he cracked, the problems he solved, the competition he beat to the tape. Listening to him you realise that he gets out of bed every morning with the same attitude as the trout fisherman tying on the first fly of the season, the jockey at the starting-gate, the actor making his entrance on opening night.

There was never a successful salesman who hated his job. The top man in selling actively loves what he does; it gives him *joy*. Why should this be? What makes selling so different from other walks of life? Well, what *is* selling? There have been hundreds of definitions of this word but they all come down to the same thing: selling is *persuading*. Creative selling is changing someone's mind. It is the situation where the salesman hears someone say: 'I am perfectly happy with what I am doing, using and buying now, and I see no reason to change'. A flat turndown, a refusal. No sale today, thank you.

The successful salesman talks to this person. He doesn't contradict him or quarrel with him or try to browbeat him or shout him down or get into an argument with him. He uses no gimmicks or tricks of the trade or high-pressure tactics; he simply talks to him. At the end of that talk the listener says something like: 'You know, you may have something there. I have never thought of it in that light before'.

Exciting! He has changed a man's mind! Someone has been persuaded, through a logical and carefully prepared presentation, that there may be a better way. How does it feel? It feels like the scream of the reel when the big one takes the hook, the passing shot in the tie-breaker which throws up the puff of white from the line, the wedge-shot which floats down, takes one hop and lands stiff to the pin.

The *joy* of selling? Believe it.

Yes, Beer, but you still haven't proved to me that I could make a living at selling. You don't realise what I have going against me. All right, let's quit stalling and look at your deficiencies, and see if any of them knocks you out of any chance of ever becoming a successful salesman. Here they are, in no particular order:

'My appearance is against me.'

I recently ran a sales clinic for the forty top salesmen of a motorcar distributor. These were the crème de la crème, the very best of the bunch. They were experienced, mature, and of course very well lined in their hip pockets since they had been in the top earning bracket for several years. They were delightful people to work with; stimulating in their participation and heartwarming in their attitude. But examined dispassionately and objectively they were really nobody's first prize. There were no tall, handsome or commanding figures among them. You would have passed any of them in the street without a second glance.

Physical appearance is no criterion of success in selling. In fact, I sometimes think that it may even be something of a drawback. If someone with a face like Paul Newman's handsome younger brother and the body of Mr Universe strides into your office you could just possibly feel threatened. If he looks like Woody Allen with a figure like a refugee from the anorexia ward there is no threat. The listener can be more relaxed and prepared to open his mind. I have known salesmen with physical disabilities – one with a port-wine stain covering most of his face, one with disfiguring scars from a motor accident – who had no difficulty in the selling interview.

Forget physical appearance. Certainly the professional salesman dresses well, is well groomed and takes reasonable pride in his appearance. But while the toothpaste smile, the Savile Row suits and the £25 haircut may get you a date on Saturday night it won't do a damn for your sales figures.

'I don't have the gift of the gab.'

It gives me great pleasure to knock this old shibboleth on the head and bury it for ever. 'Well, of course he's a good salesman,' people say. 'He's kissed the Blarney stone. He has the gift of the gab.'

Nonsense! The fast-talking, smooth-tongued salesman went out with antimacassars, the Model T, and snake oil. I don't know why some people still cling to the feeling that glibness is necessary or even desirable in a modern salesman. Again, it is almost certainly a drawback. The five hundred words-a-minute artist who crushes you with the sheer weight of verbiage is likely to get thrown out of any buying office, factory or home. A few of these characters do still exist, but they are not professionals and they never will be.

If you can put words together to form sentences you can sell successfully, and no great talent for speaking is necessary. I know a salesman with a severe speech impediment. He doesn't stutter, he just locks up solid for five seconds at a time, immobile, silent as the tomb. *Nothing* happens. Yet this man regularly goes on the overseas trip awarded to his company's top ten per cent of the sales force.

In any case, as we shall learn later, most salesmen talk too much and listen too little. You are no great orator? Okay, but you can *listen*, can't you? Then you can sell.

'You can't teach an old dog new tricks.'

One of the wonderful things about selling is that age is no handicap to starting a successful career. 'I'm too old to start something new,' is no excuse at all. It is true that not many firms are hiring fifty- or sixty-year-olds as novice salesmen, but who says you have to work for someone else? One of the big advantages of selling is that you can be your own boss.

Even less-than-perfect health need not knock you out of selling. There is a man in my home town who does very well as a property salesman. The fact that he is paralysed from the waist down seems to handicap him not at all, since he manages to sell houses very well from his wheelchair. There are salesmen who through ill-health are unable to leave their houses and who sell successfully over the telephone.

'The time is wrong to start a selling career.'

This is being written at a time when if you read and believe the business section of your newspaper you feel like putting your head into the gas oven. Times are heard, say the financial experts, and there is no relief in sight. A friend of mine who is apparently too stupid to read the business news, and who has no selling experience whatever (in fact he has no business experience, he is a land surveyor) has recently gone into the business of selling home improvements and he is well on his way to making a very comfortable living.

For the professional salesman *there are no hard times!* Now, that sounds slick, doesn't it? That's whistling past the cemetery. A tight economy affects everyone, and especially anyone involved in selling, where people are unwilling to lay out money and, indeed, don't have all that much money to lay out.

Yes – and no. Even in the toughest times products are still made, sold and bought. It is certainly true that if you are selling wood glue to a furniture factory and that factory goes on to a four-day week because of lower sales volume, then they are going to be using less glue, and anyone who doesn't see that is living in a world of his own. But what happens in that sort of situation is that the average salesman does fall by the wayside, while the professional survives, prevails and even prospers.

Wait for the 'good' times before you go into selling and you will still be waiting when they back the black station-wagon up for you.

'There are too many salesmen already.'

Wrong! There are *never* too many salesmen – good salesmen, that is. There may be too many engineers, chiropractors, bricklayers, cat-burglars or priests, but never too many good salesmen. We have been discussing a tight economy, and there is no doubt that in such a situation there can suddenly be too many architects, for instance. A man can study architecture for six years, get his degree *cum laude*, and find that because the building industry is stagnating there is no call for his services. He's good, but he isn't wanted.

This can't happen with the good salesman. He can *always* make a living, and a good one, and the hell with the financial Jeremiahs.

'I'm a woman. Selling is a man's game.'

You don't get away as easily as that, Ma'am. Selling may at one time have been the exclusive preserve of the male but those days have long gone. As I have said, I talk about 'Salesmen' in this book but that is merely a convenience of diction. Listen to me: There is no branch of selling where you are barred, simply because you sing soprano instead of tenor. You know this already. You are as smart as a man. You can hold a point in debate as well as he can. It is becoming clear from recent studies that you learn faster, drive better and stay fitter than men do. Nothing need stop you – certainly not the feeling that you have to be a sort of imitation male to succeed in selling; an original female is fine. Nor do you have to look like Rambo in drag; successful women in selling look like *women*.

I have worked with women who have succeeded in selling tractors, industrial chemicals, outboard motors, burglar alarms, life insurance, men's clothing and ethical drugs. Really the only sort of selling where a woman could be disqualified would be some product which required great physical strength to demonstrate – I can't for the moment think of what this would be.

Yes, I quite agree that there are some sales managers who are averse to hiring women, but they are a dying breed. As soon as your boss understands that you are prepared to put your heart and soul into your job; that you can grasp the basics of product knowledge as well if not better than your male colleagues; and that your customers, once they realise that you know what you are talking about, will welcome you and rely on you, you will find that you are accepted as one of the team.

*   *   *

Do you feel any better about entering the world of selling, now that we have cleared away some of the rubbish that is talked about it?

There may still be a lingering doubt at the back of your mind. You may be thinking: 'Yes, that's all very well, but if I go into selling I shall be competing with a lot of experienced salesmen. I shall be the new boy, fighting for my life against the battle-tested veterans. What chance will I have?'

Now, I am going to let you into a secret which all experienced people in selling know but which no-one ever breathes. This secret is no secret to all sales managers, sales trainers or salesmen; we all know it, we just don't talk about it. It is this: *the standard is low*. The general standard of selling is *low*. In spite of all the training courses, books, films and tapes, most salesmen out there do not sell well. I know that when I say this I am looking straight at myself since I am in the training business, but it is true. Oh, sure, there are good salesmen out in the field. There are salesmen who exhibit the highest standards of salesmanship, who are true professionals and who exalt the business of selling. I know some of these people, I have worked with them and I am proud to number them among my friends. But the vast mass of people who pick up a briefcase and go out to call on customers are not doing a competent or even adequate job of work.

Why this should be is the subject of a fascinating debate at another time and place, but the good news is that *because* this is so, if you go out there and do anything resembling a half-way decent job of work *you must succeed*.

Very soon after I started in business I discovered one of the Eternal Verities, and it has affected my whole life. It is extraordinary that I unearthed this particular tenet since I am not by nature an intellectual or even specially intuitive or deductive; however, I did. It has worked for me, it will work for you. Here it is:

No-one is ever measured by pure achievement; everyone is measured by relative achievement.

You hang on to that truth. It can change your attitude towards going into selling. You are not rated by how good you are, and don't listen to anyone who says otherwise. You are rated by one criterion only, and that is how much better or worse you are than the rest of the mob.

You can prove this for yourself if you doubt me. Do you have children at school? Has it ever happened that one of them came home beaming with pride to tell you that he got 62 per cent in a Geography test? Now 62 per cent may not sound very exciting; it isn't even two-thirds, but wait – your child was top of the class, with the next best mark only 55 per cent. Nobody cares how good you are in pure terms. A mark of 87 per cent looks fine by itself until you realise that the test was a doddle with most of the class in the nineties.

I apologise for spending some time on this simple point but it is one which very few people seem to appreciate.

The truth is that in selling you have what we could call the First Team: those guys up there sitting with the Gods on Olympus. At the other end of the scale there are the Lost Legion; those are the misfits who should never have gone into selling in the first place and who are on their way out. I don't sneer at them; selling is not for them and the sooner they leave the business and find another line of work the better for them.

This leaves the people in the broad middle band. Not as good as the stars, not as bad as the lemons: they are the vast bulk of the selling fraternity. Many of them are reasonably adequate though not inspired, but most of them are not really doing a selling job.

Why should this be? One of the marvellous things about selling which we shall be exploring is that it is a *simple* procedure. There is nothing complex about it. It can be done by anyone who really wants to succeed. Why then are there so many – let's not call them out-and-out failures, but rather – 'non-successes'?

I believe the reason is a simple but rather sad one. Look at it this way: go into the senior class in any school today and ask for a show of hands from those who intend to make a career out of selling; anyone who is going to be a salesmen please indicate. Not a single hand will be raised. Nobody has even considered selling as a way of life. Now, keep tabs on those school-leavers, and check up on them in five or ten years' time. What do you find? Several of them are in the selling business! How did this happen, when they had no idea of it when they started out?

What happens, I'm afraid, is that most people in selling at this moment simply drifted into it. They didn't start out by wanting it, it just happened. It happened – and this is the whole point of all this – because selling is still the easiest business to get into. It requires no university degree, no apprenticeship, no articles, no diploma and often, no experience to get a selling job. Try to get a position as a switchboard operator and you will find yourself under the bright lights with the Personnel Manager giving you a sort of third degree about your training and experience and references and past life and moral probity: You don't just walk into a job like that. But if you really wanted a job as a salesman and were not too fussy about what sort of selling job it was, what your product line consisted of, how well you were paid or what sort of character your boss was, you could literally be selling within twenty-four hours. So, because it is something of a last resort, people find themselves in the selling business who have no business selling.

It happened to me. After going to university more or less as a matter of course and choosing analytical chemistry mainly because my closest friend had chosen it (amazing, isn't it, how casually some of us pick out a life's work), I became tired of creating foul smells and staining my hands with nitric acid. I left the halls of academe. I took a job with the government dehydration laboratories – it was the only one available at the Labour Exchange – and for a year I watched oranges drying up and bananas shrivelling. When I could no longer stand the excitement I cast around for something else and a friend of the family reluctantly took me into his company as a salesman. Selling was therefore for me a third choice, and it wasn't so much a choice as a desperate last resort.

As it happened, it was – apart from getting married – the single smartest thing I have ever done in my life. But I did indeed drift into selling, and so do most other salesmen. Nobody drifts into quantity surveying or paediatrics or law or chartered accountancy, they plan for it years in advance. It is never a third or fourth choice.

This is the reason there are so many mediocre salesmen around, and this is why you, as a virgin salesman, need feel no doubt or diffidence about entering the selling field against the more experienced ones. All you have to do is stand three inches taller than the mob and you are king.

If it happens that you are already a salesman then for heaven's sake be big enough not to be offended by what I have said here. This is your life we are talking about, so don't get your feathers ruffled if I seem to be blunt and even brutal. I said I wasn't going to make happy noises at you, didn't I? Now hear me. You are a salesman. You probably got the job more or less by happenstance, as I did. You are earning a reasonable income although you would like it to be a lot bigger. You have read the books, seen the films, attended the lectures on selling 'techniques'. The cold fact is that *you already know how to be a better salesman than you are*. You have the expertise to be the top salesman in the team, whereas in performance you are halfway down the list.

Why?

Well, it is a truism that we like doing the things we do well and we don't like the things we do badly or, at least, not so well. Sit back for a moment and ask yourself a question which could be vitally important to you: Do you really like your job? Don't give a quick, reflex answer; really think deeply about it. Don't give the answer you have been in the habit of giving to friends and family when they asked you: 'So you're a salesman, Charlie; do you like the job?' You have been used to replying: 'Hell, yes! I like the challenge of selling. I like the fact that I don't have a manager breathing down my neck all day – they trust me, you know, and they leave me to get on with the job. Then again, I like meeting people. I'm a *people* person!'

Perhaps you don't put it in exactly those words, but you probably say something like that. Certainly, the hundreds of salesmen I have asked that question have answered in more or less those words. The point is that unless those people are good salesmen – if they are in the broad middle band of the average salesmen – then what they have said is a lot of horsefeathers and there is not a single word of truth in it. The truth is that they *don't* like the challenge of selling; they *don't* like being left alone out there to fend for themselves; they *don't* like meeting people, or at least, not the people they are forced to meet in their jobs.

I ask you again: Do you *really* like your job? Think what tomorrow will be like. Are you looking forward, as you ride into the selling arena, to the fanfare of trumpets, the clash of steel on steel, the dust and the blood, the laurel wreath on the victor's brow and the battered corpse of the vanquished being dragged away by its heels? You smile scornfully at my melodramatic description of a salesman's day? But that by itself shows that you don't really enjoy your work, because that is the way that the top salesman sees his job! All right, maybe not in quite such colourful language, but he does see each new day as a challenge, and he really feels that he is in an arena with all eyes upon him as he fights tough opposition for the prize.

If you don't feel like that then you don't enjoy your work. That's a pity, because you should. You are either in the wrong sort of selling, or you are going about it the wrong way. This book will show you which it is and how to correct it.

Whether you are already a salesman or whether you are standing on the edge of the pool wondering if you should take the plunge, the next two chapters are important, because we are now going to find out what you should be selling. Let's go.

4

*Selling isn't just selling
– what sort do you like?*

Right at this moment, someone, somewhere, is walking into a butcher shop to sell wrapping paper. He is a salesman. Right at this moment, someone, somewhere, is climbing on a jet to travel halfway around the world to sell tankships. He is a salesman, too.

Selling has to be one of the most varied professions in the world. The choice is bewilderingly wide, not only in the products or services you sell but also who you sell to, who you work for, where and how you work, and how you get paid. In this chapter we take a look at the different types of selling jobs. Somewhere here is the one for you, the one which will give you the challenge, satisfaction and joy you deserve. Hang on to your hat – you will be astonished at the choices you have.

On your own or with Big Brother?

The first decision to make is whether to join the staff of a company or whether to go it on your own.

The advantages of being one of the sales staff of an established company are many and obvious: your product line is there already, you have the backing, promotion, financial muscle and after-sales service of an organisation which is probably well-known in the market-place. You will receive training in product knowledge and also, if necessary, in selling skills. There is also the security of working for a company – although security is something which has never bothered the successful salesman very much; his security lies in his own hands rather than the whim of some senior executive, or even in the economic climate of the day. As I have said there is always work for the successful salesman. Also, the old Risk-Reward concept comes in here, as shown in the chart:

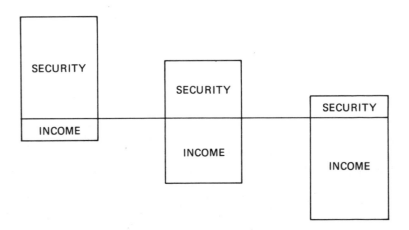

If you want a high income potential then you must accept a low job security; if you insist on job security then you pay for it by having a relatively low income. There seems to be no way out of this trap – if your company pays highly then they have a right to expect high performance from you. If you don't deliver you get fired so fast you don't have time to close the door behind you. The so-called 'salesman' who trudges around to twenty customers a day, picking up orders which have already been filled in and are hanging on the hook for him is not so likely to find himself without a job at the end of the month, but then his pay envelope has nothing in it to excite him.

If you decide to go it alone as a freelance then of course you have the happy feeling that your net profits really are net and that everything goes into your own hip pocket. You make a higher percentage profit in this way than you will ever do by working for someone else. However, and you can carve these words in marble, if you do decide to work for yourself then in order to succeed you must have a pitiless, implacable, slave-driving swine as a boss – *yourself*. Anybody who imagines that he can take it easy simply because there is no-one to tell him to get off his bottom and do some real hard work is doomed to failure. It may well get easier later on as you get established but for the first few years you *work*, friend.

When I left a secure company job to go out on my own my social life vanished, my family had to get up early or stay up late to see me and my golf clubs gathered dust in the attic. Perhaps I do work two days a week now. That is to make up for the twelve days a week I worked in the beginning.

Not to put you off working on your own but merely to point out some of the questions you will have to answer before you start:

All by yourself

What are you going to sell? Where will the products come from? Most manufacturers have their own sales teams, and while there are small manufacturers who use distributors, if their products are popular they are highly prized by the people who already handle them and are not readily available to a newcomer.

Some trade magazines do give details of lines available, or you could decide on the sort of product you would like to sell and sit on the telephone for a week phoning manufacturers of that product.

Beware of the flashy advertisements offering franchises for or huge commissions on products which sell themselves, are needed in every home, office and factory and will make your fortune in the first month of selling. If all this were true they wouldn't have to advertise for salesmen. Here again the Risk-Reward concept applies; the higher the percentage commission offered, the tougher it is to sell. I don't mean that you should automatically turn your back on a deal of this kind, but do examine the whole contract very carefully. *Especially* be very, very careful of the offer to sell you an exclusive agency for ten thousand pounds of your hard-earned savings. Go very deeply into the deal if you are attracted to something like this, get your attorney to look it over for loopholes, ask for references, ask to see other sales records of similar deals – get *everything* in writing.

Who handles the finance? Will you be responsible for the collection of money, with no commission paid to you until the order has been completely paid for? What about bad debts? And so on and so on. The money part is very important and it pays to be very picky about it before you agree to anything.

Who will your customers be? Is it a product which will be bought by business firms, government bodies, factories, hospitals or schools? Or will you be calling door-to-door on private homes? Don't knock the idea of door-to-door selling; I made a comfortable living for several years by knocking on doors. It may not be a very prestigious way of selling and the hours are terrible, but there is good money to be made if you can stick at it.

With Big Brother

How do you want to be paid? Presuming that you intend to join the sales force of an established organisation instead of doing your own thing, the very first thing to decide – long before you choose what type of products you want to sell – is: Do I want to be paid a straight salary, or do I want to get a commission on what I sell? Think about it very carefully; you may not believe it but this is the most important question in your entire selling career.

Why is *how* you are paid so important? Because the way that a company pays its salesmen dictates what it requires and expects from those salesmen.

Salesmen can be paid right across the spectrum, from all salary to all commission. Between these two extremes there is a full range of choices from a living salary plus a small commission, through a half-salary/half-commission deal, to a small retainer plus a fairly large commission.

Which do you like? Do you want the comfort of a regular salary where you always know exactly what you will get at the end of each month so that you can budget properly and plan ahead? Or do you like the idea of a salary which you can live on but which in addition gives you the potential of making a little bit more if you put in that extra effort? Or does the small retainer/ large commission deal grab you, whereby you can make big bucks and yet still have at least a part of your income guaranteed? Or do you prefer the 'damn the torpedoes, full speed ahead' concept where you get nothing at all if you don't sell but if you sell well you have money coming out of your ears?

Think well before you choose, because you are choosing not merely a way of getting paid but a style of life. Your new employers will demand different things from you depending on how they pay you. With the emphasis more on salary and less on commission they will expect you to keep meticulous records of your sales calls, submit details of carefully-planned itineraries, and generally pay close attention to paperwork of all kinds. They will expect you to work your territory fully, giving good coverage to all present and potential customers. You will be expected to attend sales meetings or have a broken leg as a reason for your absence. You may be closely supervised in the field and as you gain experience you may be asked – instructed – to take a virgin salesman out with you and blood him in the field of battle.

In a word, you will be required to be a good 'company man', obeying company rules and adhering to company policies and procedures. All this may sound daunting, but it isn't really; the sales force of a marketing company is far less circumscribed than is any other division or department in that company. In comparison with the sales side of the business the rest of the staff are part of a chain-gang. A clerk in the despatch department can't blow his nose unless he does it as laid down in the operations manual. All salesmen always have more leeway and latitude than internal staff; it's one of the things that makes selling so much more fun.

Now, as you move across the remuneration range from straight salary to straight commission you will find that there is far less emphasis on how you go about your job and far more on how much you produce. By the time you get to the commission-only deal the cry from the top is: Sales, sales and yet more sales! The straight commission salesman is to all intents and purposes his own boss in the sense that while he is bringing in the gravy he is pretty well let alone to do as he pleases. In fact if he is really doing well nobody dares to get in his way, talk loudly in his presence or thwart him in any way at all. Sales managers know that sales managers can be replaced but that the top commission salesman is a rare bird, a without-which-nothing which must be retained at any cost.

This is not to say that the salaried salesman is not expected to sell well. He usually has clearly-defined sales quotas and if he doesn't achieve these life can become uncomfortable. It is simply that the commission salesman knows he is out there for one reason and one reason only. It isn't to run surveys, make courtesy calls, give after-sales service or submit quotations. He has been hired as a selling machine, pure and simple, and while when an ordinary machine is not working properly you try to repair it, when a selling machine breaks down you get rid of it and get yourself another one.

The next chapter covers what *sort* of products you will decide to sell, but we must touch on these briefly here, because *what* you sell does to a large extent decide how you will be paid. There are exceptions, but certain products are almost always tied to certain types of remuneration. For instance, life insurance salesmen are not paid a straight salary, ethical drugs salesmen are never paid on commission. There are good reasons for this. The insurance man is such a free agent that if he were paid a salary whether he sold or not, most would simply not work hard enough to justify having them around the place. On the other hand the ethical drugs salesman calls on doctors to persuade them to prescribe the antibiotics and tranquillisers which he represents. Since he seldom takes an order from the doctor it is very difficult to work out how much product he has moved, and therefore almost impossible to pay him a commission on sales.

How many sales calls? Here's an interesting question: 'How many sales calls would you like to make every day?' Don't say: 'As many as possible, because the more calls I make the more sales I'll get and therefore the more lolly I'll make.' It isn't as simple as that. Surely, there is a direct connection between the number of sales and the number of sales calls, but the number of times you are able to sit down (or stand up) face-to-face with a listener depends largely on what you are selling. I have worked with salesmen who, every day of their working lives, make at least fifty sales calls. Think about this; could you do it? Could you be pleasant and persuasive to people fifty times a day, irrespective of the state of the weather, your bank balance, your liver or your domestic climate? Many salesmen do it and do it well, but most of us would shrink from it.

If the idea of making calls on that sort of assembly-line basis turns you off then what about a salesman I know who does not make more than two or three calls a week? He sells computer hardware – the actual machine itself – and each call can take anything from two hours to three days. Appeal to you?

Most salesmen find themselves somewhere between these two extremes, making anything from five to fifteen calls a day. This number is dictated, not by their energy or by their sales manager, but by what they sell, where they sell it, and who they sell it to. If you sell office supplies in a central city territory then you are going to make many more calls than if you sell fertilizer in a widely-extended farming territory.

High or low unit cost? Here's another option for you to mull over. (Do you see what I mean that selling offers one of the widest and richest fields of choice of any way of making a living?) Do you want to sell high unit cost or low unit cost products? This has nothing to do with high or low *price* products: we are not talking cheap or expensive here. The concept is entirely different and the distinction must be made.

Take a ten-ton truck. There is a wide range of prices for heavy trucks. You can buy a cheaper one or you can go for the expensive ones, but either way you are in the *high unit cost* business, because it takes a lot of dough to buy this sort of product.

Then, take an ordinary hose-clip such as I bought yesterday to fix the nozzle to my garden hose. The hardware store salesman offered me two types, one cheaper and one more expensive. The higher-priced clip was, he assured me, 'The best that money can buy.' Made of stainless steel, with a lathe-turned worm drive, it was unconditionally guaranteed. It was a high-*priced* product, but I paid for it out of the loose change in my front pocket, because it was a *low unit cost* article.

You see the difference, of course. High-priced or low-priced, cheap or expensive, all trucks are high unit cost and all hose-clips are low unit cost products.

Which do you want to sell, trucks or hose-clips? The man who sold those clips to the hardware store made a lot more calls yesterday than any truck salesman, and his average sale was very much lower – how many hose-clips do you have to sell to equal one truck? Before you opt for selling high unit cost products as being the easier life (hell, you don't have to work so hard, do you?) remember that the low unit cost salesman makes many, many more actual sales. The hose-clip man can sit down at the end of a day during which he has seen, say, fifteen customers, and happily page through eight or ten orders, while the truck salesman can get to the end of a week during which he has sweated blood, calling from early to late – and not have a single order to show for all his hard work.

Can you stand this? Can you accept that the higher the unit cost, the longer between orders? I once met a salesman whose quota was one sale per *year*. That's all he had to do, just sell one of his products each year. He sold executive jet aircraft. How would you like to find yourself at the end of October, with only two months to go, and still no sale? For most of us that would be Valium country. The higher the unit cost, the fewer the unit sales.

* * *

So, as you see, you have a lot of decisions to make about what *sort* of selling will suit you. Please don't say: 'That's very interesting, but I'm new at the game, and in order to get in I shall probably have to take whatever is offered.' *Don't do that.* I have tried to show that grabbing any sort of selling job is the surest way to fail in selling. This is your future, friend; take your time and get it *right*.

All we have looked at here is the *sort* of selling you want to do, and we haven't even looked at *what* you want to sell. That fascinating subject deserves a chapter all to itself.

5

Power stations or pantihose – what shall I sell?

When discussing sales training with the sales executives of a company I need to pinpoint the precise selling situation of the sales force. I ask, not so much what the salesmen sell, as who their customers are. When you enter the wonderful world of selling you will quickly realise that your selling job is best defined by who buys your products rather than what those products are.

For example, one might think that all salesmen who sell tea and coffee would have similar selling situations and problems. Their products are similar, therefore their working day will be similar: not so? Not so. Take two tea and coffee salesmen (they can even represent the same company). One sells his products to hotels and restaurants; the other sells to supermarkets and chain stores. Their products are the same *but their selling jobs are poles apart.* Why? Because of the use to which their customers will put their products. The hotels will be *using* the tea and coffee while the supermarkets will be reselling it. That's the vital difference. If I am buying a product from you to use myself, my point of view is quite different than if I were buying it in order to sell to someone else. Your sales presentation to me will have to be quite different in its turn.

The interesting thing is that if we now look at the salesman who sells soaps and detergents we see that if he sells his products to supermarkets he has a very similar selling scene to the beverage salesman who also sells to those customers. If on the other hand he sells his washing powder to hotels he hoes a similar row to the coffee salesman who also sells to hotels and restaurants.

So *customers*, not *products*, dictate the selling situation. Thus the first queston you have to answer before even you decide on the type of product you like, is:

End-user or reseller?

Do you want to sell your product to the person or company who will actually be making use of it, or do you prefer the idea of selling to people who will display your product in stores to sell to others at a profit? Choose carefully; the difference is chalk and cheese.

End-user selling. Here you could be selling to factories, offices, hospitals, schools, government and municipal bodies, or private individuals. The people you talk to are purchasing officers, engineers, storemen, office managers, home-owners or company executives at all levels – anybody who has the authority to buy something which he or his organisation can put to use in some way.

Sometimes it may seem that the line between end-user and reseller selling blurs a little. If you sell a company your power units and they build them into their air-compressors which they then sell, is this end-user or reseller selling? In fact there is no problem; it is still end-user selling because they don't resell your power unit, they *use* it to build their compressors. It is their product that they sell and not yours. This may sound picky, but let's get it right.

The end-user salesman often works through appointments with his customers. Compared with his reseller colleague his interviews are more leisurely affairs and they take longer. The end-user salesman has to have excellent product knowledge, since people buy his product to use, and usually need to have very precise and specific details of how it will suit their requirements. The good end-user man goes around with his head full of the minutiae of torque curves, flash-points, colour-fastness, toxicity, vitamin E content, fire-resistance, tensile strength and drawbar horsepower. End-user customers are much concerned with after-sales service, parts availability, guarantees and standardisation.

[38]

Reseller selling. Here your customers would be supermarkets, chain-stores, pharmacies, and shops of all kinds. The people you see are departmental buyers, chemists, store owners and managers. The reseller salesman is right out there in the marketplace. He usually calls on his customer in his place of business, the shop or store itself. The reseller salesman sells standing up. He has to compete for his buyer's attention with the people who are in the shop to buy, not to sell. Who do you think the customer will want to attend to – the people who want to give him money, or the character who wants to take it away from him? I have had customers in a store interrupt me to comment unfavourably on the product I was trying to sell and, damn it, on my sales talk!

Reseller salesmen usually make more calls per day than the end-user man and the calls are shorter in duration. Also, he has a double selling job to do. When he has sold his products to his customer he then has to help him to sell them to *his* customers, by means of display cards, tumble-packs, gondola end specials, counter stands, check-out racks and all the other mysteries which come under the umbrella heading of Merchandising – which simply means the promotion of the product at the point of sale.

Many salesmen believe that reseller selling is the poor relation of end-user selling; they find it beneath their dignity to get into a pharmacist's window in their socks to set up a display of shampoo. In fact, the reseller salesman's job can be exciting and stimulating. He wouldn't change it for the end-user man's job where, as far as he is concerned, nothing much happens from one year's end to another. He knows that in the highly competitive world of reseller selling the whole marketing scene can change dramatically from day to day – even from morning to afternoon.

Reseller salesmen don't have to know as much about product ingredients or performance as end-user men; a grocery buyer doesn't care about the exact percentage of sodium stearate in the kitchen soap. However this doesn't let the salesman off the hook. He *does* have to have a very good working knowledge of how his customers' businesses operate, of 'wet' demonstrations, of optimum product display at eye-level, of shelf pressure and impulse-buying and so on and so on.

Customers of the reseller salesman are much concerned with advertising back-up, special deals, continuity of supply, delivery times, co-operative promotions and stock-room space. The salesman must be able to talk about these on the same level as his customer if he is not to waste the customer's time – and lose his respect.

That is the difference between end-user and reseller salesmen. You can see it was well worth the time we spent in discussing it.

Sometimes a salesman has to wear two hats and be all things to all customers. This could be the case if you sold, say, adhesives and the territory isn't big enough to support two salesmen. You could find yourself selling industrial adhesives to factories in the morning and consumer adhesives to hardware stores in the afternoon. Nothing against this, so long as you understand the reasons behind the sale in each case, and that they are often diametrically opposed to each other.

So, on to a look at some different industries and products. Somewhere here is the selling job for you, but first a word of warning. It may be that your hobby is photography. You are knowledgeable and enthusiastic about zoom lenses, f-stops, enlargers, filters and emulsions – so why not sell photographic equipment? Surely with your knowledge and enthusiasm you are half-way there already!

Maybe – and maybe not. Certainly you could talk to the owners of camera shops in their own language, and you could quickly learn the strong sales points of your product range. The problem is that there is a world of difference between happily playing around with your cameras as a pleasant, weekend hobby, and having to get out of bed every morning of your life and sell the damn things. I don't say that if you have an abiding love for scuba diving, playing the trombone, bonsai or restoring Victorian houses that you should not seriously consider selling these products, but don't automatically pick your interest or hobby and assume that you will be happy if you turn it into a career. The moment something becomes compulsory where before it was voluntary it is a very different scene. Amateur is amateur; pro is pro.

Here we go:

Automotive

There is a feeling that the car salesman has it pretty cosy. After all, how tough can a job be where all you have to do is sit in a showroom while people walk in and buy? It doesn't work that way these days of course; the successful car salesman picks up a briefcase and goes out looking for business in just the same way as any other field salesman. The reason for this is that the really big business in automotive selling is fleet sales where you sell to a business organisation – not one car at a time but five, ten or twenty. This means making calls. Since transport managers see no reason for calling on you, you have to go calling on them.

When a customer buys a new car he usually has an old one to trade in, so the pro motorcar salesman has to have a good idea of trade-in values. This isn't as difficult as it sounds; all car salesmen have a little black book which gives average values for used cars, or some of the bigger companies have a valuator who does nothing else.

A sound knowledge of how a motorcar works is a tremendous help in selling cars. You don't have to be able to strip and repair an automatic gearbox, but you should know the principles of automatic transmissions. I know that many car salesmen will tell you that they sell very well without knowing what goes on under the bonnet. After all, most customers don't have any knowledge or interest in the works department of their cars, so why bother? Maybe so, but true enthusiasm for a product comes from confidence in that product, and product confidence comes from product *knowledge*. Write it in letters of fire.

Selling used cars is rather looked down on; I don't see why. There is the stereotype of 'Honest Joe's Junk Car Emporium', with honest Joe resplendent in sideburns, a loud checked suit and a bowler, offloading jalopies to unsuspecting victims. If he still exists, Joe is in the minority; most used car firms are attached to full franchised car dealers and they are proud of their reputation.

The truck salesman has a rather different job from the passenger car man. He has to have a far deeper knowledge of his products from a technical point of view, and horsepower ratings, fuel efficiency, maximum loads and dual axle design should roll easily off his tongue when required. He should be familiar with the laws regarding commercial vehicles, and these are complex. He must of course be in possession of a heavy vehicle licence and be competent to drive the entire range of his products. This is why truck salesmen tend to look down on the passenger car salesman, believing him to be the Flash Harry of the automotive world.

The truck and car business has its ups and downs as does any other but perhaps it is affected by the prevailing economic climate more than most. This is capital goods business, after all. People tend to put off buying in hard times, preferring to stick it out with the old model 'until things get better'. This means that the average salesman can find it tough to make a living, although the top salesman still seems to keep on selling. I don't say that most car salesmen are a lazy bunch of layabouts, but it is true that if you are really willing to give it everything you've got, it is not too difficult to shine in this business; it is probably one of the quickest ways to make good money.

Automotive salesmen are paid on a low-base, high-commission arrangement.

Fast-moving consumables

Under this heading come foodstuffs, cosmetics, over-the-counter medicines (non-prescription drugs), stationery, and anything which is bought, used up quickly, and bought again. This is reseller selling, of course, and your customers are those listed in the section on reseller salesmen. Here, as I told you, you are right in the front line. It can be a very exciting type of selling because you are deeply involved with new product launches, special offers and all the ramifications of merchandising your product. You attend meetings where the advertising division and their agents lay out promotional strategies and give you the ammunition to move your product on to the shelves of your customers. You are fighting tough competition which is doing its best to blow you out of the water while you are doing *your* best to sink them without trace. And the whole marketing scene is very flexible and fast-changing.

Talk to an industrial salesman and he will probably curl his lip and tell you that the consumables salesman is really no salesman at all. After all, if you sell one of the big household names in, say, toothpaste then the grocery buyer has no choice but to stock your product. His customers will expect to find it on his shelves and will give him headwind if it isn't there. So where is the selling? This is true only as far as it goes. How much of your product he buys, where he puts it in his store, how co-operative he is about in-store demonstrations and special displays – believe me, this is all creative selling.

As far as the national chain stores are concerned it is true that the actual initial sale is probably done by a senior sales executive of your company at very high level in the head office of the chain, but there is still plenty of selling to be done by the salesman in each branch of the chain.

Fast-moving consumables salesmen are usually paid a living salary, with sometimes a relatively small commission or incentive bonus if they sell well against quota.

Pharmaceutical

This type of selling is divided into two distinct sections. On the one hand we have those medicines which do not require a doctor's prescription, such as vitamin pills, some analgesics, antacids and many cough preparations. These are known as 'OTC' (over-the-counter) products. Since they are sold to chemists they fit into the fast-moving consumables section just dealt with. The other type of pharmaceutical selling has to do with prescription drugs and is a very different scene. Here you would be calling on doctors, specialists and dentists, to talk to them about your drugs and persuade them to switch their prescribing habits to your products. Except in the case of 'dispensing' doctors – usually those in remote areas – and veterinary surgeons, no physical sale is made; that is, no order is taken. This leads some people to think that the call on a doctor is not strictly a sales call at all. In fact the call is often referred to as a 'detail' and the ethical drugs salesman is known as a detail man.

I dislike the term 'detailing'; it sounds as though all that is involved is an *explanation* of what the drug consists of and what it is intended to do. Nothing could be further from the truth. The top salesman in this field knows very well that he is in a tough, competitive market, and that when he enters a doctor's surgery he is there to make a creative sale.

There are literally hundreds of pharmaceutical companies, all trying to get a slice of the pie and hold that slice once they are established, and the doctor has an incredibly wide choice of drugs for almost all the ailments he treats every day. The thing is that there are very few 'unique' drugs on the market. Almost every drug available today has many competitors which will do a very similar job of curing diseases. For instance there are at least a dozen diazapam tranquillisers offered, and as for broad-spectrum antibiotics – well, you can read yourself to sleep with the varieties offered.

The salesman who calls on doctors is exactly that; a *salesman*.

You might find this type of selling truly fascinating. You have a product range that you can really get your teeth into and you are constantly kept up to date with innovations and discoveries in the field of materia medica. It is no drawback if you don't know an anti-tussive from a beta-blocker. You are given an intensive course in product knowledge which by itself is a most interesting experience. Most drug companies prefer to hire their salespeople from outside the industry and train them from scratch, so lack of experience is no handicap. On the other hand – and this applies especially to women – some very successful drug salespeople have come from the ranks of the nursing profession. Incidentally the training course entails some very hard brainwork, so if you boggle at the thought of going back to school for a couple of months then don't even think of this as a career.

Some ethical drug salesmen go around with a built-in inferiority complex when they call on doctors. The doctor has spent many years learning his craft; how can you, with only a couple of months of learning, be anything but a waste of time to him? This is silly. The doctor doesn't expect you to have a medical degree. What he does have a right to expect is that you know every single thing about the product you are talking about, that you are able to answer questions about dosage, serum levels, contra-indications and side-effects. So long as you don't try to teach the doctor his job he is usually prepared to listen to you. In the ethical drug business you will have the shortest sales talk of any salesman; if you get a full ten minutes with a busy doctor you are doing very well indeed, and five minutes is more usual. In that time you must get across everything about the drug which you are highlighting that month, and it isn't always easy.

Think about this field of selling as a way of life for you; many salesmen find it a most rewarding and interesting business. If prestige is important to you, there seems to be a certain status to this job compared with selling door-to-door, for instance.

Pharmaceutical salesmen are always paid straight salary or, just possibly, high-base, very low commission.

Industrial

This is a very wide field. The industrial salesman can be selling anything from coated abrasives (that's sandpaper, Mabel) to heavy machinery; from very low unit cost to very high. He is called an industrial salesman, predictably, because he sells to industry, and his customers are factories and manufacturers of all types. He is of course an end-user salesman.

If you like messing about with argon-arc welders, rust-proofing compounds, drill presses, routing machines, polyurethane coatings and crankshaft grinders then industrial selling is for you. I say 'messing about' because any good industrial salesman can be identified at the end of his working day by the sawdust in his hair, the paint on his hands, the grease on his pants and the chalk on his shoes. The successful man in this field carries earplugs, protective goggles, and a hard hat in his car and spends part of each day with his sleeves rolled up.

If you are at all technically-minded then industrial selling can be the greatest job in the world for you. You are talking to engineers and technicians of all sorts. These people are traditionally conservative in outlook but while they often tend to cast a jaundiced eye upon salesmen, if you cut out all the bull, never try to be something which you are not and above all, don't overclaim for your product, you will find that they respond to you.

The industrial salesman is first and foremost a problem-solver. That is what his products are intended to do – to solve the manifold problems in a manufacturing or processing plant, on a building site, a land-clearing project, a road construction project, a dam-building contract. Every one of these jobs has problems of one sort or another, and every single plant engineer, site foreman or construction boss wants higher production, less downtime, ease of maintenance, worker safety, technical backup, quick turnaround – you name it. Give him these, and do it without any smart-arse, gimmicky, high-pressure tactics, and you will be welcome time and time again.

You will sometimes sell by tender where complex quotations have to be submitted, and here you could be dealing at the highest level, with government, county and municipal officials. One of the fascinating aspects of industrial selling is that you could be peering into the bowels of a turret lathe with a workshop supervisor in the morning and then have to scrub up and miss lunch so that you can appear before a tender committee in the afternoon. You work at all levels.

Your remuneration as an industrial salesman could span the range, from straight salary to high-base, low commission, or small retainer and high commission. As a rule though, in the really high unit cost products you tend to be paid more on the salary side than by commission. It makes sense, you see; if you are selling something requiring very large outlays you could go several months before you tie up a sale – and in the meantime your family is digging for roots to eat. Pay is good for the good industrial salesman, and his company hangs on to him; he is hard to find.

The building trade

Companies who sell to the building industry are really in the industrial field, of course, and much of what we discussed in the previous section applies here too. I have separated this section because there are certain specific aspects which the ordinary industrial salesman does not find in his work.

If you sell flooring, additives for concrete, shuttering, aluminium siding, plastic sheeting or guttering you could be selling to building contractors or even homeowners, but you could also be calling on architects and consulting engineers – and here is where the difference comes in. The architect or engineer doesn't buy the product from you, he merely recommends it or specifies it. You will recognise that this sort of selling is very similar to pharmaceutical work, since you do not take a direct order but persuade the listener to recommend, specify or prescribe the product for use by others.

This is straight salary remuneration because of the very high unit costs involved; if your special windows are specified for a high-rise complex you could be talking in millions.

Softs

Clothing and allied industries are usually called the softs. This is closer to the picture of the old-fashioned type of 'drummer' than probably any type of selling. The clothing salesman climbs into an estate car piled to the roof with skips full of samples, and he calls on clothing shops and displays his wares. He is the 'commercial traveller' of many years ago. His strength is his in-depth knowledge of his customers and their business. He knows what they sell and what they are likely to buy from him to the extent that he can almost write out the order before he walks in. In high-density areas he is likely to work out of a showroom where his customers will come to make their choice, but in the country districts of course he goes to see them. This means a lot of travelling, so don't think of this as a career if you like to sleep in your own bed most of the time.

The softs man needs a sound knowledge of fabrics and fashions. I have even known a salesman to do some basic designing of the trimming of clothes to suit a particular customer and have them made up by his factory.

This is low-base, high-commission selling and it is very seasonal. The softs salesman works like someone possessed of a demon for six months in the year and pumps iron or does his macramé for the rest of the time.

[47]

Door-to-door

I suppose the archetypal picture of the door-to-door salesman with his ingratiating smile, breezy spiel, cracked shoes and yesterday's shirt is what has put so many people off the idea of selling as a career. It is true that there is still a good number of these characters around, selling everything from potato peelers to magazine subscriptions. But it is equally true that the successful door-to-door man can make himself a lot of money very quickly indeed, with a minimum of product training and no apprenticeship at all.

Only last month a young woman knocked on my door, smiled, scared the hell out of me by painting a vivid picture of what would happen if I had an electrical fire (I live in a very old house), demonstrated her fire extinguisher, took my money and her departure – all in eight minutes. I later did a quick survey among my neighbours and figured that she must have had a call to sales rate of two to one. This means fifty calls, twenty-five sales. It also means she must have been earning about twice as much as the mature and highly-sophisticated computer bureau salesmen I had been working with that week. Oh, yes, you can make money and plenty of it selling door-to-door. That clerk who tells you contemptuously that he had another of those 'pedlars' knocking on his door last night is possibly not making enough to pay the 'pedlar's' income tax.

What do you need in order to become a successful door-to-door or 'direct' salesman? Two things only, both essential.

You must have a product which people really want or need. I really needed a fire extinguisher – so do you, so does everyone – I simply hadn't got around to buying one. The product should have something special about it (which is why this sort of selling is often called 'speciality' selling). Either it should be something not readily available in shops, or it should be the sort of product people don't normally go out to buy. Also, it should be easy to understand, so that you don't have to spend half-an-hour (which the listener won't allow you, anyway) explaining the thing.

Choose a more expensive, quality product rather than a cheap and nasty type. Three reasons: first, you will be more confident when selling a good product – you won't have to try to fake your feelings about it. Second, people are generally more prepared to fork out money for obviously good-quality products at the door than for something which looks as though it will fall to pieces before you can get out of the gate. Third, your commission per unit sold is higher on a more expensive article!

The second essential for successful door-to-door is moral courage. You won't find this claim in any other book on selling, but it's true. Most writers and speakers on salesmanship seem to gloss this over but I promised not to make happy noises at you, and I tell you now that you do need a goodly share of plain and simple guts if you are to succeed in door-to-door.

Let's spend a moment on this. Why is courage more important to a salesman who calls on people in their homes than to one who calls on business organisations? They are both dealing with people. What is the difference between calling on Mr North in his office or Mr South at his factory, and calling on them when they are at home? I suppose it is that at work they *expect* to be visited by salesmen. They see it as part of the job they are paid to do and in fact it is probably true to say that they could not do that job so well if salesmen did not call on them. They need the information which salesmen bring to them about new products, procedures and ideas, all of which help them in their work. At home they don't *need* to see salesmen. This is their time for relaxing, not for listening to sales talks and making decisions about buying.

This is what has worried you about door-to-door when you have considered it as a way of making a living, isn't it? If so, there is a certain validity in your concern. Speaking as one who has done a good deal of this type of selling I can assure you that when you first pick up your briefcase and start out, that innocent residential street or that harmless apartment block can assume a frightening aspect. Arrogant, brusque, offhand and even belligerent monsters lurk behind every door. You need courage, buddy.

The truth, and every successful door-to-door salesman will testify to this, is that 999 people out of 1000 are not actively unpleasant. They may be busy or not interested or even afraid of you (yes!) but I can't recall one really nasty incident in all the thousands of calls I have made on people in their homes. I do remember with pleasure the many interesting people I met, the many, many profitable sales I made and the lovely lucre I earned in door-to-door.

For this type of salesman especially does the Golden Rule apply: people tend to treat you as you treat them. Try to con them, show no consideration for the fact that they have invited you into their homes and that you have the common responsibilities of a guest, give them the third-degree or the high-pressure treatment and you will find yourself outside so fast it will take your breath away. Show a genuine confidence in your product, a real desire to help, and a quiet cheerfulness of manner, and you will be amazed at how nice people can be.

It still takes guts, though. Make twenty calls and get twenty turn-downs and it takes a withdrawal on your supply of courage to ring the twenty-first doorbell. This is why so many salesmen who do well in conventional selling would scream in horror and head for the hills if you suggested that they change to door-to-door.

There is no prestige whatever in this sort of selling, if that worries you at all. No prestige, no title, no name on the door. Just money.

All door-to-door men work on commission only.

The 'Party' method

An interesting sort of speciality selling has become very popular in the past ten or twenty years; it is the Party method. A prospective customer is persuaded to ask her friends to come around to her house to listen to salespeople and inspect the products of a certain manufacturer. Plastic containers, waterless cookware, cosmetics and household linens are among the products which are sold this way, and the list is growing.

It is an interesting way of selling and it can be very effective. The Party guests often tend to open their purses because of a sort of group excitement – or simply because they want to impress their friends. The hostess is usually given a discount on her own purchases or a free piece of product as an incentive for running the party. There is a feeling that the Party method has been over-used, but many companies are still doing very well by it and indeed require no other method of moving their products.

Life insurance

Hey, you – come back here! Don't skip this section! Don't say, as thousands of salesmen have said: '*Not* life insurance. I could *never* sell life insurance.' At least hear me out. If you don't, you could be missing out on one of the most effective ways of making good money in selling.

Why is it that so many salesmen, or people who would like to get into the wonderful world of selling, are scared stiff at the prospect of selling life insurance? It's not difficult, you know. No, really, it isn't.

I worked for four hours a day for three years and made a perfectly good living selling life insurance. I did not lose any of my friends (which is one of the crazy reasons put forward for not getting into insurance), and I had the bittersweet experience of delivering three cheques to widows which they all urgently needed after the unexpected and world-shattering deaths of their husbands. Had it not been for my calling on those husbands and persuading them to buy insurance those women would have been in serious financial trouble.

When a life insurance salesman delivers his first policy cheque he becomes an instant believer; he is a knight errant and his rate-book is his morning star.

Be careful to distinguish between life insurance (which is more correctly life assurance) and what is known as 'short-term' insurance. The latter is insurance against fire, theft and so on. It covers property rather than lives. The short-term man is employed by his company and is usually on a straight salary scheme. The life insurance man is more properly an agent of the company and is almost always a commission agent or more rarely, a low-base, high-commission man.

Think about life insurance as a selling career. Don't be put off by any horror stories you may have heard or preconceived notions you may be harbouring. Here is the truth about this interesting and unusual way of making a living. The bad news comes first.

Only one man in four makes a success of life insurance; the other three give up after a year or even less. This leads people to believe that it is a very difficult type of selling, and this simply isn't so. The truth is that the wrong people go into insurance. At least, people go into it with the wrong attitude.

[51]

This is the easiest job to get into in all selling – you could, quite literally, become a life insurance agent tomorrow morning and be selling it tomorrow night. To be brutally honest, this makes life insurance the last refuge for some of the biggest misfits and bums in the whole selling business. It's a pity, but it's true, and it doesn't help the image of the professional life insurance man.

You are completely on your own in life insurance. You get very little help from your office except some basic preliminary training, and this consists mainly of showing you how to use a rate-book and fill in a proposal form. Most of the sales training I have seen in life insurance companies is primitive. It tends towards the slick and gimmicky and is best forgotten. There is no company-paid car or expense account.

The final bit of bad news is that even your own colleagues are in opposition to you, and this must make it unique in the selling business. There are no sales territories as such; it is every man for himself. And although there is an unwritten law that you don't poach on another agent's customers, as the old cliché says, unwritten laws are not worth the paper they're printed on.

The good news about selling life insurance? Well, you are selling one of the biggest bargain offers of all time. After all, what are you telling people? 'If you die before your time we will give your family all this money – thousands of times more than you have paid in. If you live to a ripe old age we will give you back all the money you paid in and much more. You can't lose. Also, this is the only contract you will ever sign which is strictly one-sided, because we can never cancel it; only you can do that, any time you want to.' What a bargain! What a wonderful thing to be able to sell!

Then again, while most other salesmen have a limited market for their products (you can't sell lawnmowers to eskimos), the insurance man can walk down any street and there are his prospects. Anyone who is healthy and between the ages of one day and seventy years. They are everywhere and everybody. They are either so poor that they can't afford to be without insurance or so rich that they have to protect what they have.

These days, life insurance salesmen are by no means restricted to selling life insurance, oddly enough. The modern retirement annuity schemes, pension augmentation plans, and so on have widened the range of products which the insurance salesman can offer. He is by no means going around 'talking about death', which is another silly reason given for shying away from this field as a means of livelihood.

You choose the hours you wish to work. You choose the people you wish to call on. The job has a snowballing effect, so that it gets easier with each person you sell to.

Think about it.

Service selling

There is a type of selling which can be put under the heading of Services, where you don't sell a product as such. Your company *does* something for your customer. Window cleaning, pest control, gardening services, renovating, security guards, home improvements, tree surgery, telephone answering; there are hundreds of companies engaged in these pursuits and they all need salesmen to sell them.

I have never been able to understand the salesman who says: 'I couldn't sell an intangible; I have to have something I can show and demonstrate to the customer.' I have sold both tangibles and intangibles, anything from bulldozers (which are about as tangible as you can get) to annuities (nobody ever *saw* an annuity) and for the life of me I can't see that it should be any more difficult to sell one than the other. As for saying you can't demonstrate an intangible, well, if the salesmen now making good pay out of selling factoring and debt-collecting and loss-of-profits insurance and computer services didn't demonstrate their services they would soon be looking for another line of work.

Service salesmen are paid across the range from straight salary to straight commission.

Property

I give the selling of property – houses, flats, and commercial properties – a section to itself because it has two unusual aspects which make it different from other selling. In the first place this is one branch of selling where you can sit for examinations and put

some letters behind your name to show that you are a professional. In the second, property selling is unique in that you have
to go out and find something to sell before you can go out and sell
it. It's true that people do walk in and ask you to sell their houses
for them, but you can't rely on that. Half the estate agent's job is
persuading people to let him sell their property; the other half of
course is selling that property, which is the part that pays him.

The property business pays straight commission, or sometimes
low base/high commission.

*   *   *

There you are: some of the types of selling you can get into. The
list is not exhaustive and you can widen it by looking through
trade directories and glancing at the jobs offered section of the
daily paper.

Take your time about deciding on your field in selling. Don't
listen to people who tell you that times are hard, jobs are scarce,
and with your lack of experience you had better grab the first one
that is offered – that's a lot of nonsense. You already have a job.
You are not desperate. You are in no hurry. This could be the
biggest step of your life, so walk around it, savour the idea, talk it
over in depth with those close to you. Get the *feeling* of it.

This does not mean that you are being half-hearted about
entering the selling business. You are not saying: 'Well, I'll give it
a try and if it doesn't work I can always go back to hot-dip
galvanising.' When you make the change you are going to do it
with all your heart and all your effort, with excitement and with
joy. Just make every reasonable endeavour to be sure it is the right
pool you are diving into.

Don't look for a job in selling – look for the selling job which
will give you the money you want and the joy you deserve.

COFFEE-BREAK 1: IS IT JUST THE MONEY?

Every now and then we are going to break away from the heavy stuff in this book, gather around the coffee machine, and chew the fat about this and that in the wonderful world of selling. Here's our first coffee-break.

I have been talking about the 'successful' salesman, and it may be as well to sit back and ask just how one judges whether or not any person (not only a salesperson) is a success.

Is it just the money he has in the bank? Silly question; I doubt if anyone reading this uses only the criterion of money as an indicator of success. If this were true then Albert Schweitzer was a drop-out, Vincent van Gogh was a lousy painter, and Mother Theresa has made a complete mess of her life.

However, before we get too cosy about how money isn't everything, how it is the root of all evil, how it doesn't bring happiness, and how life is too short to spend it chasing money, let's have a little chat about that long, green stuff, shall we? Always a fascinating subject.

I am up to here with the losers who sneer at people who have made it in the material sense; those men and women who through their own efforts have accumulated an honest pile of the world's wealth. In most cases this sneering is simply sour grapes. The losers haven't made it, so to excuse their failures they dredge up all the old clichés to hide their shortcomings. Heed what follows, because if you are to become a successful salesman it may well be that in the process you could just get yourself a nice chunk of filthy lucre. (Except isn't it funny how when we get it ourselves it ceases to be filthy and miraculously becomes as clean as new-fallen snow?)

[55]

Let us expose some of the nonsense that has been said and written about money, and in the process get rid of any guilt feelings you may have about going into selling in order to live a little higher on the hog.

Money isn't everything

Of *course* money isn't everything, just as fame isn't everything, health isn't everything, married bliss isn't everything. Nothing is everything, but money can be a very pleasant part of the whole. The man who tells you that money isn't everything has envy in his heart. Have you noticed how quick the failures are to point at the man with money who slips up in any way? Ooh, how they love it! See how they read every word of the messy divorce case where a millionaire is involved!

Some years ago two rich men were tried and convicted of illegal business practices. In fact, they had merely been doing what lots of other people were doing – they made the mistake of being caught at it. The details of the case were very dull and, to the layman, obscure and difficult to follow. Never mind – every day of the trial the public galleries were full. The failures had come to gloat at the fall of the titans.

Money is the root of all evil

This piece of nonsense must share with the saying 'A little knowledge is a dangerous thing' the prize for being the most misquoted in the language. the truth is that nobody ever said anything so idiotic. The correct quotation is 'The *love* of money is the root of all evil,' which is a very different thing. It comes from the letters of St Paul to Timothy, and Paul was much too intelligent to have said anything so fatuous as 'Money is the root of all evil'.

Certainly, money can be used in evil ways and it often is. Indeed, an obsession with money can destroy a man's soul; but abuse of a thing has never been an argument against that thing.

Money doesn't buy happiness

This has to be one of the most stupid things ever said by man. It is stupid and it is wrong, because the truth is that in many, many cases money *does* buy happiness. You shake your head. Beer has gone overboard on this one. All your life you have been told that money can't buy happiness. You have probably said it yourself many times. It has become one of the world's most hallowed axioms. Yet it isn't true now and it never has been. And you can prove it to yourself right now without leaving your chair. Think of three people you know who have money, and three who don't. Wouldn't the three without money be happier with it? Aren't the three with money happier than they would be without it?

Money has of course no supernatural powers. It can't bring the dead back to life, solve complex psychological problems or rebuild shattered families. Yet it can give security, decency, confidence and dignity to people who don't have these things and who desperately need them, and if that isn't a solid foundation for happiness it will do until one comes along.

'Ah,' people say. 'Look at those who are wallowing in money and who are still not happy – what about them?' So? That proves nothing. the jet-setters who spend their lives on the couches of fashionable psychiatrists, the so-called beautiful people who can't build a single meaningful relationship, the celebrities who OD on hard drugs – these were losers anyway. Because money has the effect of accelerating and dramatising events it probably hastened and intensified their problems, but they would have been failures with or without it.

Yet this tired old tag about money and happiness still finds its way around. I knew a man who started a business in a rented back room and who by sheer damned hard work made himself a millionaire. Then providence played a particularly dirty trick on him; the wife he adored was struck down by an incurable disease which turned her in early middle age into an old woman. His love for her was a shining and beautiful thing and his feelings for her never changed. Would you believe that some creep once said about him: 'Well, all his money can't buy *him* happiness!'

Setting aside the motives behind that remark (things said by people like that are dried goat-droppings blowing in the wind), let us examine the remark itself. Money could not restore that woman to a normal life, that is certain. But it could buy the expert day and night care, the privilege of living out her remaining years in her lovely home with its beautiful garden where she could be wheeled out to sit in the sunshine. It bought him the freedom from having to leave her to earn his living. It allowed him to spend all his time with her – I once saw them sitting quietly together and holding hands. Please don't tell me that his money didn't buy them happiness.

Life is too short to spend it chasing money

This sounds plausible, even laudable. Here, we say, is a sensible man, one who has his priorities right. No way is he going to bust a gut in a frantic search for financial success.

Indeed? Well, you examine this man carefully and you will find that he is not busting a gut being successful; he is busting it being a failure. His alarm clock throws him out of bed every morning so that he can fight his way into work where he is Assistant Despatcher for the Scroomall Manufacturing Company. He spends his whole day doing boring and soul-destroying work full of petty and irritating details, taking instructions from people he hates and fears. He says that life's too short to spend it chasing money, but the truth is that his failure is actually making his own life shorter.

It is well documented medically that the 'ulcers of success' idea is in fact a myth. People get ulcers, migraines and a host of psychosomatic illnesses, not from succeeding but from failing. Doctors' waiting rooms are full of people who have been passed over for promotion, who fear retrenchment, who have slowly but ineluctably felt the clammy grip of failure around their hearts, who have realised that the ship of success has pulled out and left them on the quayside.

What do others say about money?

We can assume that while you are not obsessed with the idea of making money to the exclusion of everything else, you have no objection to some of the lovely stuff sticking to you as you take on a selling career. If you still harbour any guilt feelings about making money, look at what some people have said about it.

Samuel Johnson said: 'There are few ways in which a man may be more innocently employed than getting money.'

Shakespeare said: 'He that wants [i.e. is short of] money, means and content is without three good friends.'

George Bernard Shaw said: 'Money is indeed the most important thing in the world, and all sound and successful personal and national morality should have this fact for its basis.'

Richard Steele (1684) said: 'No doubt, affluence is a blessing, notwithstanding the frequent perversion of it, or else it had never been made the subject of so many divine promises.'

Albert Camus said: 'It's a kind of spiritual snobbery that makes people think they can be happy without money.'

Michael Beer said: 'If you want money, go for it, mate!'

Can all these great brains be wrong?

Enough; you might be looking for the sort of joy in your job which does not include dipping your bucket into the money river. I have tried to show that in many cases money is merely incidental to success in selling. What you have to bend all your efforts to is finding the job in selling which gives you what you want, and you may want many things, only one of which is money.

No, the answer to the title of this coffee-break is: of course it isn't just the money. But if you *do* want to make money then for St Agnes' sake don't feel *guilty* about it. There is nothing unethical, anti-social or naughty about making as much money as you want.

6

How do you start?

You have decided that selling is for you. You have taken that deep breath, maybe poured yourself a double instead of the usual modest single, raised your glass to yourself, grinned at your image in the mirror, hugged your loved one, and you are ready to take the divine leap into space. Excelsior!

Whereupon the music fades and dies, the cheering crowds drift away and the labourers begin to take down the bunting, because you have no idea what to do next.

Here's what you do.

Let us assume thay you intend to join an established company rather than go it completely alone, where you have to carry your own lines, do your own accounts collecting and everything else. In spite of all the obvious benefits of being your own boss my recommendation is that you join a company as a member of the sales force, at least to begin with. Let them handle the marketing and finance so that you can concentrate on becoming a successful salesman. When you have found your feet you may decide to leave them and go on your own – or you may decide that you are very satisfactorily placed right where you are.

If you happen to find the right products falling into your lap at the very outset then by all means try the independent route, but for most beginners the gateway to successful selling is through a company.

If you have the thought that it isn't ethical to join a company knowing that you may leave it in a few years then please lose it. If the company doesn't suit you or if your goals should happen to change in the future, you will leave, right? Well, when the company hires you it is with the thought that if you don't suit the company, or if its goals happen to change in the future, it will fire you. So what's the difference? You are not marrying your boss, you are merely working for him while the arrangement suits both of you. He understands this and so should you.

All right, how do you get a selling job? I have promised to be honest with you and not to pretend that something is easy when I know that it is hard. If you have never sold anything before then it is true that you may come up against a classic Catch-22 situation: many companies won't hire you unless you have already had experience as a salesman. Of course the way to get experience as a salesman is to be hired by a company as a salesman . . . Round and round the mulberry bush.

I have met many would-be salesmen who have come up against this situation and have given up in despair. Don't. Yes, there are many companies which hire only experienced salesmen. You see advertisements reading: 'Only salespeople with at least seven years' experience in selling maternity wear need apply'. This is a stupid advertisement for reasons which we needn't go into, and the person who created it is going to miss out on a lot of good people. But you do see a lot of this sort of thing. I don't believe that I should be very happy about joining a company such as that one anyway. It is a sure bet that they don't have much of a training programme for their salesmen if they want them to come already trained (that's what the advertisement means).

Okay, forget them. Don't apply for the job and hope that when the interviewer sees your honest, eager, intelligent face that he will immediately say: 'My boy, I don't care if you have no experience whatever, I am so impressed by you that you have got the job!' This happens fairly regularly in the romantic magazines, but we are in that tragicomedy known as the real world, and here it doesn't happen.

Go instead for those companies that deliberately hire people who have never sold a thing in their lives. Believe me, these outfits do exist and there are plenty of them. They don't want salesmen from other organisations coming into their sales teams with preconceived ideas, with old habit-patterns already built in, with reluctance to learn new policies and procedures. Most executives don't react too well when the new boy says: 'Well, of course, in the Vertical Sales Company we did it *this* way.'

No, they want virgins in the selling business. People they can start right from square one and in whom they can inculcate their own special way of selling their own specific products. I recently ran a management clinic with twenty managers from thirteen widely-varying sales companies, and when I asked: 'How many of you would be prepared to hire people with no selling experience at all?' twelve of the twenty put up their hands. In the subsequent discussion it came out that seven of the managers actually *preferred* to hire brand-new people. They went out of their way to get school-teachers, clerks, artisans and men and women in jobs similar to these. I have one client company which hires only school-teachers! Another sales manager I know seems to concentrate on bank-clerks. 'They seem to be well-organised people,' he says. 'They have a sense of responsibility, and of course I can pay them a lot more than they get in the bank, so I can pick the best.' Fine.

What sort of company? From previous sections you have a pretty good idea what sort of products or services you would like to sell. Before you start applying for a job you have to decide what sort of *company* you want to work in. Do you want to be part of a big company, or do you prefer a small crowd? Do you want the excitement and glamour of a growth organisation, or the solid dependability of a consolidation-minded company? Here follows the good news and the bad news of each sort – take your pick.

Mickey Mouse or King Kong?

In a small company (small in the sense of not having a large staff) your light can shine very brightly. You are closer to the corridors of power and the people who walk them. You are more visible. There is a much more personal atmosphere, and the rules and regulations, the bureaucratic bull, is much less evident and much more flexible. There is far less danger of your being hidden away in some backwater where you will be the invisible man – never noticed and never promoted. If titles are important to you then the small company provides them much sooner; it is much easier to become as Executive Vice-President of Mini Motors than it is of General Motors.

The other side of the coin is that in a small company there is simply not the wide *variety* of selling jobs going. Also – and this put me off 'family'-type concerns for good – where the whole show is literally owned and run by one family, you could find the son of the boss brought into the firm, given a thorough grounding of a fortnight in the accounting department and three days out at the plant. Armed with this vast experience he has become your immediate superior! Be very careful of the sort of company where your name is not the same as the one on the brass plate outside. Even the brilliant Lee Iacocca found problems in this situation, and it was not even what you could call a small company.

In the big national companies the field for promotion is wider, the staff training facilities are better, and the really top jobs are very attractive indeed. Also, and this could be very important, the good big companies are continually looking right across the board at everyone on the payroll, to find the slots which suit them best. You could find that out of a clear sky you are offered a job completely different from the one you occupy, because the computer hiccupped your name out when senior management was seeking a person for a fascinating, lucrative job which had just opened up.

Against all this is the fact that because of its size, people can get lost in the labyrinths of the organisation. Promotion can be slow because of the numbers of hopefuls clamouring for attention. Or at least, when the promotion does come it can be less dramatic than in the smaller concern. This need not worry you if you are determined to give the job all you've got. Have we not already recognised that the overall standard is low?

There is one aspect of big business which must be mentioned here. In the big ones the threat of office politics, interdepartmental bickering and general 'do unto your neighbour before he does unto you' feelings and atmospheres do exist. Some people can't live in this sort of climate, but others love it.

Ask yourself how you would stand up to a situation where your colleagues walk with flick-knives up their sleeves and brass knuckles in their pockets. When it comes to five people gunning for that one plum job you have no friends. Your confreres are ambitious, they want the same recognition and advancement that you do, and no quarter is expected or given. Old Charlie on your team is a helluva nice guy around a couple of snorts on

[63]

Friday night but when it's a question of you or him he is quite likely to smile in your face as he shoots you in the guts.

I guess I must have been too soft for this sort of guerrilla warfare because it was one of the reasons I pulled out of line management and went off on my own. But you may revel in the cut-and-thrust. (Yes, of course I've exaggerated the situation, but it does exist, all the same.)

Beanstalk or Buckingham Palace?

Oversimplifying a little, companies can be classed as those which are mainly interested in a rapid expansion of the business, and those which are more or less as big as they are likely to get. The latter are more interested in consolidating their position in the industry, streamlining their production, rationalising their efforts, and raising their profit margins. (Any management consultant would sneer at those definitions but we are salesmen and they will do for us.)

To a large extent, whether or not a company is growth-oriented is determined by the particular industry it participates in because there are growth industries as well as growth companies. At the time of writing this, computer software is a growth industry, building materials is not.

I would lean towards a growth company for you in your first go at selling as a career. There are any number of very fine consolidation-minded companies; the major oil companies are a good example. They treat their people well, and of course they have all the staff facilities you could wish for. But they are are not noted for dramatic promotions or sky-high salaries, at least not at the level you would be entering them. On this point, don't forget the risk-reward rule; the higher the reward, the higher the risk. Civil servants aren't fired easily but they don't get paid much, either. Advertising executives have money bursting out of cardboard cartons, but if they lose a big account they don't even bother to go back to the office. The man who complained that his job security was so low that his name was on his office door in chalk with a damp sponge hanging next to it, was earning a lot of money.

Right! You have, I hope, decided to join a fairly big company and one which is more growth-oriented than statically inclined. Now all you have to do is find the one which is waiting to hear from you. How do we do it? Let us count the ways.

Rat-tat-tat-tat

Simplest of all ways to go about getting a job (of any sort, not only in selling) is to knock on doors and ask for one. It requires no writing, phoning, preparation, reading advertisements or any- thing at all except a clean shirt and a close shave. How simple can you get?

Don't do it. I say this with the full knowledge that a friend of mine did exactly this and collared himself an absolute dream job; still I say, don't do it. Sure, you may just be lucky enough to hit the right person at exactly the right time, but the chances are not good, the averages are against you. Worst of all, you could wreck your chances in that company for good. Approaching them in more conventional if not so dramatic ways you could stand a much better chance.

I'm not being snobbish or superior when I say that there are jobs which you get by knocking on doors, but the sort of job you are looking for, in the sort of company you want to work with, does not hire its salesmen that way. Now just to show me, why don't you go out and get that dream job after ringing three doorbells? I don't say it isn't possible, but then it is also possible that the rich uncle in Alaska who you didn't know existed will leave you a million – it just isn't very damn likely, that's all.

Likely or not, why not try it for the hell of it? There is a very good reason why not and it is this: what you would be doing is nothing more or less than door-to-door selling, with yourself as the product. While there may be nothing against this on the face of it, remember that you are brand-new at the business of selling. If you don't get quick results from this exercise (and as I have said, the over- whelming chances are that you won't) you will get depressed, you will lose the enthusiasm which got you to change your life-style in the first place, and the real danger is that you will give up right there before you have even got started. That would be a tragedy.

Help wanted

The most obvious way of getting a job in selling (or indeed, any job at all) is to look in the Jobs Offered section of the daily papers. Thousands of jobs are advertised and thousands of people are hired in this way. Go ahead, buy all the papers and look through every advertisement. Don't just do it for a day or two, make it a regular exercise for at least a month.

Then when you have done this we'll try something else, because you may well have wasted your time.

The problem with answering advertisements for jobs is that is *is* the most obvious way. That is why everybody does it, and why it so often doesn't work. You are being trampled to death in the rush of hopeful applicants, that's the trouble. Instead of being out there on your own. I don't say that you won't get your dream job from an advertisement; the best job I ever had I got by answering an advertisement and fighting twenty-three other applicants for it. You may do exactly the same thing. Look in the Jobs Offered columns by all means, but while you are doing this you will also be doing something else which will give you a much better chance.

Yours faithfully

The method we are going to examine now works. You may not like the look of it very much, you may feel that it is a real waste of time and effort, but it works. If my life depended on my getting a job and I was allowed only one way to get it then this would be the way I would choose.

As to why this way works, let's look at an analogy. I once asked a very successful life insurance salesman for the secret of his success. He said: 'I suppose that the big difference between my colleagues and me is that they all go out and try to sell insurance to people who are thinking of buying insurance. That's fine, except that every other insurance salesman is also calling on those people. Now, I call on people who have no idea of buying insurance; that way, I'm the only insurance man calling on them.'

This is what you are about to do. Instead of applying to the companies who want to hire salesmen you will apply to those who have no idea of hiring salesmen. It may sound crazy, but at least I guarantee you won't be killed in the stampede!

It isn't as crazy as it sounds. You will be approaching the bigger rather than the smaller companies, remember. These people are on a fairly constant look-out for new talent – especially the growth companies, and that is where you are headed anyway. One of the biggest problems of any growing organisation is getting good people. They never really stop looking, even if they are not actually advertising at that time. In any case, and this is something that not many job applicants realise, a lot of companies *don't ever advertise for people*. Many of the companies I work with have told me that they have given up advertising as a way to get new staff. Why? Mainly because of the poor *standard* of applicants produced in this way.

So you will go for the companies that are not advertising, just as my insurance friend goes for the people who apparently have no need of insurance.

We have decided that you won't walk up to their place of business and knock on the door. Very well, what about telephoning? It's simple, it's easy on the shoe-leather, it's a cheap way to get in touch with a lot of people in a relatively short time, so why not give it a go? Sit down with a list of the sort of firm you want to join, phone them, ask for the personnel manager, the sales manager, the product manager – whoever, and make your pitch.

There is really only one thing wrong with this idea. The reaction you get will either be, thanks for calling but we don't need anyone right now, or, thanks for calling, but why not write us a letter? The problem with the telephone as a way to get employment is that it is too easy for the person you are talking to to release himself from the call. All he has to do is say thanks but no thanks, and put down the phone. Because he has no immediate need for a salesman (or rather, because the need hasn't been thrust at him by some immediate circumstance) and because when you called he was probably busy with something else, his automatic reaction was to get you off the line.

Which, finally, gets us to his suggestion to you: why not write him a letter? We are going to do it without the unnecessary preliminaries of knocking on his door or dialling his number.

You go through trade directories, the business section of the paper, you talk to the local chamber of commerce, you look in the Yellow Pages – whatever. You make a list of thirty, fifty, a hundred names of companies of the sort you want, selling the products you want and of the size and – where you can find it – the business philosophy you want. Then you write thirty, fifty, a hundred letters. That's it.

Oh, I know it's a sweat, it's a nuisance; how are you going to get that number of letters typed? How do you know whether they want salesmen this month or even this year? Sure, a lot of them won't even answer the letter, and those who do will for the most part send a curt, three-line turn-down. Quite right, all of those objections; but this is what you are going to do and this is the way you will probably get the job you want. Believe me, of all the ways to try for a job in selling, this is the one to bet on. Let's examine the objections to this multiple-letter plan and see if we still feel negative about it.

It's a sweat to type all those letters. Yes, it is. Not only typing the letters, but hell, think of sticking all those stamps on the envelopes! This objection carries weight only with the person who approaches the idea of changing his life with the same attitude as the man who is buying a pair of socks. If you quail at this point then my advice is to give up the idea of becoming a salesman; you don't want it enough.

Who is going to type all those letters? Well, if you don't type well yourself then get professional help here. Go to a copy-typist (they are in the 'Services Offered' section of the paper) and get her to do the job properly. She will have a good-quality electric typewriter, which is also a must. This is one situation where you don't want a word-processor for the work – at least, not one of those where the printout is composed of little dots. This looks a little too much as though you have had a hundred letters typed, and we don't want that now, do we? Yes, it will cost you something to use the services of a typist; so, have peanut butter sandwiches for the next few days in preparation for the *filet mignon* you will be able to afford when you get your new job.

How do you know whether they want salesmen now or in the immediate future? You don't, and a lot of the people you write to won't. There is always wastage in the direct mail business – which is what you will be engaged in when you send out these letters – but it still works in some circumstances better than any other form of selling. You do understand that you are now engaged in your first selling job, don't you? You are selling that precious commodity – yourself.

A lot of the companies won't even answer the letter. Right, and those that don't can be taken off your list. You don't want to work for them. *Good* companies always answer every letter, no matter how much of a nuisance it may be. If it isn't junk mail it gets answered.

Even those companies which do answer will probably just send a brief turn-down. Yes, a lot of them will. In fact most of them will. It could be as high a figure as ninety-five per cent refusal, which means that you would get only five interviews out of all those letters. Let us say that again slowly, and this time let us understand exactly what we are saying: *from the letters you write you will get five interviews for the selling job you want.*

Now that we realise what a great way this is to go about grabbing that job which everybody wants, we are ready to look at the letter which we are going to write. But before we do, it strikes me that we glossed over one of the objections rather too quickly.

It is true that the vast majority of firms which you approach will not want any more salesmen right at the moment you write to them, but this does not mean that you won't get an interview. As I said, most of the bigger companies are constantly on the lookout for talent, and they will interview people all the time, whether or not they have a slot that needs filling at that moment. You could very well get the reaction from such a company: 'Thank you for coming to see us. We do not have a vacancy at this time; however, we believe that you could fit into our sales division very well, and we would like to keep your name on file and get in touch with you when a vacancy does occur.' When a good company says something like this they are not merely putting you off; this is not the 'Don't call us, we'll call you' turndown with a sugar-coating. If they tell you something along those lines then it's pretty sure that they mean it. And *that* means, my friend, that you have got a job – there is a delay before you actually join the team, but you are *in*.

I know that we are jumping here, but I want to stay on this for a moment while it's hot. If, as and when the above happens to you, thank the person warmly and go home. Then write him another letter, thanking him for the interview, expressing your appreciation of his favourable reaction and saying how much you are looking forward to hearing from him. In the meantime, you say, you would be grateful if he could let you have whatever product literature and other information he believes would be useful to you. This will serve you in two ways. First, it will impress the hell out of him, don't think it won't. He will realise that you are not playing games, that you really mean it about joining the company, and this will put you on the inside track of anyone else who might be on their list for a job in the future. Second, when you have got the material from him and gone through it you will again be ahead of the rest of the pack. When the time comes for the company to hire a salesman you will probably be asked to come in again for a final interview, and think what an impression it will make if you can make some points about the products you have studied!

If you really want to put your interviewer into shock, show him that you have not only studied the material which he sent you but you have also taken the trouble to go out and get some information on products and companies which are in competition with the interviewer's. I promise you, nobody has ever done that in this man's experience, and if he doesn't fall out of his chair with surprise and delight then walk out on him.

People don't *do* the sort of thing we have been talking about, so when someone actually does do something like this he very quickly becomes the only one on the short list. Remember, the standard is *low*. Stand just the tiniest bit taller than the rest of the mob and you are king.

But of course, none of this will be possible unless the letter you write gets you into the interviewer's office, so let us quit stalling and look at the letter.

7

The application letter – the 'Open sesame'

Here are some thoughts which might help when you compose your letter:

1. A touch of class

This letter is *you* on the interviewer's desk, so let's do it with style. We have already said, good quality typewriter (and a good quality typist). Make it decent paper, too, not that stuff that they sell in blocks as 'typing paper'. Use at least a good 100-gram stock.

2. It's a letter, not *Jaws V*

Most letters of application are too long; keep it brief, punchy, readable. The man who gets your letter isn't interested in what colour belt you wear in Karate. He wants to know who you are, what sort of job you are applying for, and what makes you think that you could do it. Oh, sure, put in married or single, children or still trying; that takes only a line or two. But the letter which gets read is the one which gives him the three pieces of information mentioned above and gives them to him in a shorter form than *Gone With the Wind*.

3. It's the best policy

It's a great temptation to paint the lily in your letter. You are
assistant to the office manager? Well, let's just leave out the 'to
the' when describing our present job, shall we? Assistant Office
Manager sounds much better. Don't do it. Ethics has nothing to
do with this advice. Your little bending of the truth will eventually
be found out, and it could wreck your chances completely.

In a big company you will at some stage of the interviewing
chain find yourself in front of the personnel manager. This character is always on the lookout for the little white lie, and he works
on the theory that if someone will lie about a teensy-weensy thing
then he is a liar, period.

4. Make it sing!

There has to be something in your letter which sets it apart in
some way, which makes it unusual, memorable, *special*. The best
way I can describe this special quality in a letter of application is
to quote from memory from some letters which have stuck in my
mind – and the fact that they *have* stuck in my mind is a good
indication that they were indeed unusual.

Now for the love of Pete don't copy these extracts word-for-
word into your own letter. These are not your words; they are the
words of others. I give them only as examples:

'I am writing to you because some time ago I talked with a
member of your staff, and I was impressed by his enthusiasm
for the company. I believe that a company which can produce
that sort of attitude in its employees is the one I would like to
work for.'

'I have taken the trouble to find out some things about your
company. You seem to have a particularly good image in the
eyes of the public and this is obviously important to you. I
would like to be a part of that.'

'There is really no reason why you should hire me as far as my
experience goes since I have no background of the type of

selling you do, but I am really interested in the sort of e
ment you carry and I would learn quickly.'

'All I would bring to the job would be plenty of energy and the
knowledge that I have a lot to learn. Would this be enough to
start with?'

'After reading the article in Fortune magazine about your international operation I showed it to my wife, and she said: "That's
the sort of company you have always talked of joining." I think
she is right.'

That sort of thing. Sit back and ask yourself: What would make
me take a second look at a letter of application? Why would I
decide to see that particular applicant?

Don't be facetious or flip in your letter, don't be smart and
don't be cosy. Don't use a single exclamation mark, and on the
heads of my children I implore you, don't be funny.

It may be useful to you to glance at the headings I list below
when drafting your letter. I'm not going to write it for you and this
is not laziness on my part. Your words have got to be you, not a
carbon-copy of someone else. There are books on the market
which tell you how to write your own CV (*curriculum vitae*, if
you didn't go the classical route at school – it's a pompous term
meaning, literally, 'the course of one's life'). You may care to page
through one of these manuals and even buy it. My own feeling is
that at least for this preliminary letter where you are making the
first contact with a company, it isn't necessary and may well even
be dangerous to put down everything in your life, back to where
you won the Show-and-Tell prize at the age of seven. The long-
winded resumé is all right if the company has asked for it, but this
is a cold approach from you, and you want it to be *read*. Here's
what to get in it, and damn little else, please:

- Type of position you want.

- Why you want it.

- Why they might want you for it.

- What you have been doing up till now (keep it very short).

- The sting (make it special).

[73]

You realise that while the body of the letter will be the same for all the letters you will be sending out, the sting may well be different for each letter, depending on what you want to say to make it memorable, interesting and specific to that particular company.

Right; spend some time on the draft, polish it, take out anything which contravenes the few don'ts which I mentioned above. Then line up your typist and let her rip. But wait! Here she is, sitting at her typewriter with plenty of good-quality A4 paper and the draft of the letter. She has a list of a hundred company names. She runs the first sheet into her machine and says to you: 'Who shall I address them to?'

That is a damn good question, isn't it?

Well, you could address it to 'The Sales Manager' because he is after all the guy you want to get to, isn't he? There is only one problem, and it sits outside his office and goes through his mail and it throws out letters addressed to 'The Sales Manager'. It is called a private secretary. All right, she doesn't always throw them out, but a letter addressed to a title and not a name is not very special, is it? And this letter has to be special. How to get his name? Well, Benjamin Franklin said: 'If you would learn something – ask someone.' What a brilliant, if somewhat unconventional, idea!

Two ways to do this: by personally calling on the company and asking the receptionist, and by telephoning and asking the switchboard operator. In neither case do you want to see or talk to the big man's private secretary (personal assistant, as they call them these days) because there is no way she will give you the name of her boss without a thousand words, and you don't have time for a thousand words.

It sounds like a lot of bother to call personally on each of the companies you want to write to and it is. The only time you would be likely to do this is if they are all located in a small area, or if you wanted to case the joint before deciding whether or not to write to them.

The telephone is by far the best bet. In most cases the girl at the switchboard will want you off her case as quickly as possible. She will tell you the name and cut you off in the same movement. Fine, but sometimes they will ask: 'Who is calling, please?' And even: 'In what connection is this, please?'

Resist the temptation to tell her that it is none of her damn business. Merely say that you are writing him a letter and you have to make sure you spell his name correctly. Actually, you should never have exposed yourself to 'Twenty Questions'. When I want the name of an executive I act busy, harried, and hurriedly polite but not deferential. It goes like this: 'Good morning. I am going to have to write to your sales manager, and I need to be sure of his initials and the right spelling of his name. Could you help me on this?' The 'I am going to have to' makes it sound businesslike and routine – no big deal. If she does ask who is speaking I tell her: 'It's Beer here – Michael Beer Associates,' and after that I have no trouble. The fact that there is no such organisation as Michael Beer Associates is neither here nor there; it makes her happy, I get the name I want, and no blood is shed.

You have your hundred names, you have sent out your hundred letters. You are waiting for the five per cent positive reaction which will give you the five interviews which will give you the one job which will change your life.

Go ahead, walk through that door and charm the hell out of the interviewer – in the next chapter.

8

Beating the Star Chamber
– how to win in the interview

It is most likely that when you are granted that interview you will be told when to present yourself, and no discussion is invited or expected regarding the time. However it does sometimes happen that you will get that much longed-for call and be asked if Thursday is convenient and what time would suit you? If this happens *don't*, I beg of you, start getting all polite and say: 'Why, any time at all; when would it suit *you*?' I know it sounds very gentlemanly but it is not the way to go. You say firmly: 'Thank you, ten-thirty would be fine for me, if that fits into your schedule too.'

This is telling him that you are both busy men, that you both have pretty full schedules, but hey! It looks as though you have found a time which suits you both. Saying that any time at all is okay with you also tells him that you don't have a thing in the world to do. Who wants to hire someone who is sitting around, smiling and scratching, while the world goes by him?

And now we are ready for the eyeball-to-eyeball. At the risk of insulting your intelligence I must remind you that if your clothes look like an explosion in a paint factory and your hair is as long as her mother's visits then you will certainly qualify for a job – but not everybody wants to be the barker outside a strip-joint. Same applies to you, ma'am – don't be offended, but while he may love looking at cleavage as a fully-paid-up member of the male persuasion, he doesn't want it under his nose while he is deciding whether or not you will enhance the image of the company when you call on its customers.

I hate to admit it but I once turned down a likely candidate for the sole reason that he had a touch of lipstick on his shirt. I don't know and don't care whose it was – perhaps his mother kissed him for good luck – but if he was as sloppy as that for an important interview, imagine what he would look like on a routine call to a customer.

Here are some pointers to remember during the interview, and if any of them seem elementary, kindergarten stuff – well, it's the little things that count.

Don't try to kiss him

Don't be over-familiar. *Don't* stick your hand out at him; he may not be a shaker. Be very ready if he puts his paw out at you, but let him start it. Treat his desk like an altar-cloth, just in case he is one of those people who would rather have you blaspheme his household gods than touch his desk. Don't put your briefcase or hat or even your hands on it. Don't be loud, don't laugh too much, even when he cracks a joke.

It's sweeter than music

Use his *name*. Oh, Saint Agnes, how important this is! Make sure you have his name, make very sure you know how to pronounce it correctly and use it, easily and naturally. People get very teed off if you keep calling them 'you'. And these days, 'sir' is stilted and fussy in a one-to-one interview. This is no small point; using his name makes the whole interview more personal and more memorable for him.

Remember that one thing is in his mind from the start to the finish of your discussion with him: 'If I hire this character, how well will he get along with and across to my customers?' When I was in the business of hiring sales staff I never let this question go far away from my mind.

[77]

He won't shoot you

Don't be too nervous; the result of this one interview will not affect the destiny of the human race. You can't crack every nut in the bag and why should this interview be the one that works for you? Note that I said *too* nervous. You will be a little tense and that's a good thing so don't fight it. At the start of the big race the racehorse is a little tense. If he isn't then don't bet on him. A cow in a field is never tense, but then, cows don't win races.

However, if you are too nervous this will transfer itself to the interviewer. Any attempt to hide it merely makes things worse. What is likely to happen then is that he will believe that you badly need the job, and in most cases this puts people right off. This is an odd thing: he will not mind in the least if he sees that you very much *want* the job – dammit, that's why you are there. But he must never feel that this job is your last resort, that it's this one, or the suicide note and the rope on the beam in the woodshed. He may feel sorry for you, but he won't hire you. His job is hiring successful people, not running a Salvation Army depot.

Tell it like it is

Give full yet concise answers. If he asks: 'Why do you think that you will fit into this company?' don't smile weakly and mumble that it seems to be a good company and you generally get on well with just about anybody. He wants a reason, so give him a reason: 'I believe that a salesman has to have faith in his product range if he is to sell it successfully. Your marketing strategy is obviously to occupy the upper range of quality and price in your industry, and I think that I would be comfortable with that sort of selling philosophy.'

Who's interviewing who?

The good interviewer is well aware that there are two interviews going on here. He is trying to find out as much as he can about you so that he can make a decision, but he never forgets that you are trying to find out enough about the company to be able to decide whether or not you want to join the outfit. Any manager who doesn't believe this is not the sort of guy you want to work with. Again, the trained interviewer knows that he can find out a hell of a lot from you simply by the sort of questions you ask him, and he is keen to hear those questions.

So, ask the right questions. Here are some examples of questions which I have had thrown at me by applicants for a selling job. See how you would have reacted if you had been in my place:

- What are the working hours?
- If I leave the company what happens to my pension fund?
- Do I have to work overtime?
- What sort of company car do I get?
- Does the medical aid include dental expenses?
- Would I ever be transferred?
- How many days leave do I get?

How would you feel as a manager if you were asked these questions? Well, none of these heroes got the job. But surely these are important questions. Doesn't the applicant have a right to know the answers to them? Certainly, and he should not take any job without getting answers to at least some of them. (Come on, now, one or two of them are pretty infantile.) But these questions and their answers should come much later, when you are much closer to getting the job. If you ask these questions at the first interview you are saying, loud and clear: 'I'm not looking for a job, what I am after is sheltered employment.'

The right questions should show that you want to fill the job properly, contribute to the prosperity of the company (and, therefore, your own – no-one minds that as a reason), and at the same time be accorded the recognition you deserve as a worthwhile member of the team. I am almost frightened to put down examples of the right sort of questions for fear that you will learn them off by heart and parrot them at the interviewer. (No, of course you wouldn't do that. I am talking to the guy sitting next to you.)

'I wonder if I could ask you something before we start. I have a good job now and I don't want to jeopardise it. May I be certain that my approach to you will be in the strictest confidence?' You want to know this, of course, but it does no harm to remind him that you are not on the dole but do have a decent job already. Companies like to hire people who are already employed.

'What sort of staff training would I be exposed to, and is it an on-going thing throughout the company?' This shows him that you are looking ahead and that you expect to be part of a company development programme – and that you are not afraid of learning.

'I have to be sure that I could fill the job. Do you have a job specification that I could see?' Believe me, this will impress him; not one applicant in a hundred asks to see the job specs – but it is one of the most useful guides to you as to whether or not the job is the sort of thing you want.

'Looking ahead, I should like to feel that I had a chance of moving up in the company when I had proved myself. Do you have a policy of promoting from within the company?' An important one, this. You don't want to be heading for that plum job only to find that they have brought some clown in from outside and put him over you.

'Who would my immediate superior be? What is his position in the company?' The answer to this one tells you better than anything else just where *you* would stand in the organisation.

This sort of question, introduced at the right time, produces exactly the right impression in the interviewer's mind. He sees that he hasn't merely got another chancer who is desperately looking for a job – any damn job, just so it brings in some money – but a professional, someone who knows just where he wants to go and just how to go about getting there. You don't ask the questions as though you were giving him the third-degree; he won't stand for grilling from a job applicant. But showing him that you have thought deeply about joining this particular company, that you have prepared for the interview and that you have certain specific points which you would like to have cleared up –

all this must put you on the inside track when it come weeding out the probables from the possibles.

What else can I tell you about the interview? Well, don't be afraid of the catch question. Many interviewers like to stick in a question or two to put you off balance. They don't necessarily do this for laughs or to show how clever they are, but for the very good reason that they're considering you for a selling job. In selling you are going to find plenty of customers who will throw really tough questions at you to put you off your stroke. Your interviewer merely wants to see how you will react under a little pressure.

When he throws one of these at you, take your time, smile at him to acknowledge that the question is a little out of the ordinary, and answer it confidently. If it shows some small drawback in your qualifications or background, something which could make you slightly less of a prime candidate, don't worry about it; it doesn't mean that you have been knocked out of consideration. I have hired I don't know how many salesmen, and of all of them I can only remember two who were absolutely suited for the job in every possible way. All the others had some failing or lack in their experience, technical background, age, linguistic ability or whatever. I hired them because the goods outweighed the bads, and that is how you will be hired, too. (Want a laugh? Neither of the two 'perfect' candidates lasted more than a year.)

Interviewers like to ask questions such as: 'What did you like about your last job?' Or: 'What didn't you like about your boss?' These are known as open-ended questions, since they cannot be answered with a plain yes or no but need a full answer. Don't say: 'Well, there wasn't really anything I didn't like about him,' because this is what he is waiting for, and the next question will be: 'What are you doing here, then?' Something like this is what he wants: 'It was not so much a question of my not liking either my manager or the job, but I felt that I had abilities and self-motivation which the job didn't call for. Also, while I liked him as a person, it did seem to me that he lacked the skill of delegation; he tried to take on too much himself. There I was, only too willing to take on a bigger load: it was a little frustrating.'

That will show him that you have no idea of knocking your ex-boss or your old company (which is the certain kiss of death, so don't ever try it); however, it gives a good, logical reason for your move.

[81]

It may seem that I am advocating the asking of questions for the sole reason of impressing the interviewer. Not so. This is your future career we are talking about here, and you must know what you are letting yourself in for. It is a dangerous philosophy to say: 'Oh, well, let's get any job in selling for a start, just to get a foot in the door. Once we are in we can look around and find something better.' That is not the way to go. You do not want a track record of short-term jobs because this is the sign of the compulsive rambling rose. People shy away from you if it looks as though you can't hold down a job.

Examine the job carefully and thoroughly. No company will hold it against you for not leaping into the first job offered to you. Remember that it won't do them any good to hire you, spend time and money on training you, and then lose you after six months when you find that the job after all is not what you want. This is not a contradiction of what we said in previous sections about joining a company and then, a good deal later when you have a solid background of experience, leaving to go it alone.

At the end of the interview, be positive, courteous and efficient. Thank him for seeing you, but don't go overboard on this; you are being courteous, not servile. Don't forget to ask him when you will hear from him – something like this (your words, not mine!): 'The job sounds interesting and challenging, and I believe I could do it. Could I ask when I can expect to hear from you?'

If you have not heard from him within a few days of the time he has given you it is quite in order to phone with a courteous enquiry, but don't whatever you do call around in person. The 'I just happened to be passing and I thought I'd pop around' approach is not professional.

Lastly, don't try to play one company against another; it doesn't work and it could blow up in your face. Implying that if they don't grab you, IBM is ready and eager to snap you up will get you a horse-laugh and a quick brush-off. On the other hand if you have seen several companies and you do get a firm offer from one of them, it does no harm to phone the others and tell them, as a matter of courtesy, that you have been offered a job elsewhere, that you are accepting it, and that you appreciate their considering you. You never know, one of them might ask you to come in and see them again before you finally decide. If this does happen, my friend, then you are really dealing from strength. It has often happened that a firm offer from another company has made this one stop dragging its feet and reach a decision. And the job may be better than the first one offered.

This is not playing one against the other, it is merely considering which of two offers suits you best, and it has cost you only one phone call. It's worth the little extra effort to do this sort of thing! It seems to me sometimes that people approach the buying of a used car with far more dedication, research and effort than they do the changing of their lives.

Have I made the point that during the whole interviewing scene you are not in a master/servant, boss/slave relationship with the interviewer? You are two professional business people who have got together to see whether you suit each other. You don't go hat-in-hand; you are not asking for charity. You are not of course supercilious, overbearing or arrogant – but don't be bloody *humble*.

You may like to put on paper a list of the questions he may ask you, so as to be prepared for the tough ones. If you do then here are some possibles. Knowing more or less what you are going to answer does help some people. Then again, some say no, I don't want to do that; if I prepare in advance my answers are going to come out as though I had learnt them by heart. Here they are if you think they will help – I found that they did help me when I was job-hunting:

- Why do you think you could do this job?

- You seem to have had several jobs in the past; are you having difficulty settling down?

- You have no experience in our rather specialised industry; how will you manage to cope?

- We were thinking of a somewhat younger/older person for the job. Aren't you a little old/young for it?

- Isn't your present company a good one? Why do you want to leave?

- Isn't your real reason for joining us the fact that you would be earning more money?

- We supervise closely in the field. Do you think you could stand having someone breathing down your neck?

Oh, no; don't look here for answers to those questions. They would be my answers, and we want yours, not mine. Also, you may prefer to put down your own questions – maybe these are not what you believe will be asked of you.

So! You have done all you can to prepare for the interview. You are looking good. You have given yourself plenty of time to get there. You know exactly who to see. You are confident but not overconfident, and, I hope, just a little tense. You have nothing whatever to lose from this interview, and everything to gain. You are looking forward to it – it could be interesting and even exciting – and it could change your life. Go for it!

A final word. George Bernard Shaw's first book was turned down by fourteen publishers. Fred Astaire's screen test produced the reaction: 'Can't sing, can't act – dances a little'. Robert the Bruce's spider fell on his head seven times before he made it. Edison had literally hundreds of failures before he found the right filament for the light bulb.

Get the message?

PART 2

Winning in the
wonderful world of selling

9

Sell and enjoy!

Right! You have secured your selling job. You are part of the sales team of a reputable company, one with a good growth record in the industry of your choice. You already know something about the products you will be selling and you will be learning a lot more. You have a good grounding in company policy and procedure, and you are learning to fight your way through the sea of paperwork without which no self-respecting business organisation would dream of operating.

Now you have to learn how to persuade your prospective customers to buy what you sell.

In fact, long before now you will surely have begun to delve into the skills of creative selling. It you have any self-motivation whatever you will have spent some time on Part Two of this book before Part One helped to get you the job which you were seeking. In a way, therefore, this book is the wrong way around; there wouldn't be much point to your going to all the trouble of turning your life upside down and getting a selling job, only to find that you don't like selling. I had to do it this way, though. I tried to do it the other way and it didn't work, as you will see if you try reading it like that. Having written it this way, however, I fully expect you to read it right through before you make a single move towards scrambling out of the comfortable rut you have occupied for so long.

How much preparation should you do before you go for the job you want? That is, how much of Part Two do you need before you work on Part One? Do you try to become a fully-fledged ace salesman before you find a job? No, of course not. But how far do you go down that road?

THE JOY OF SELLING

I am often asked by would-be sales people whether or not they should take one of the many sales courses available from professional training groups, Technicons or university extra-mural study programmes. My answer, and don't forget that I am in the training business, is usually: 'Don't waste your money.' This is not to knock sales training – the business has given me a good living for too long for me to foul my own nest – but the point is that when you join a *good* company it will put you through its own training programmes. Why use your money when you can get trained for nothing? And more important, it will be training which is specific to the company's products, customers and selling situation.

Yes, but you want to impress your prospective employers with your initiative and drive. You would like to be able to tell them that you have attended a sales course to help prepare yourself for the job of selling. The problem is that the sales executives of most companies seem to prefer their staff un-defiled by other philosophies of selling. They want them to go through the training prescribed by them, and to use the methods which the rest of the team uses. Oddly enough, they don't seem to mind so much if they see that the applicant has been doing some reading in the field of selling; in fact, they often see this as an indication of a wish to improve oneself. I remember being much more impressed when I was told by an applicant for a job that he had spent his leave working in a temporary selling job, than if he had put down several hundred bucks of his own money to attend a selling course.

Anyway, you and I are committed to spending some time together right now, preparing for the time when you will go out and do battle in the selling arena. We are going to be looking at the art of selling. While there are literally hundreds of books, tapes, films and courses on selling, what we are about to do is different from them all in two significant ways. First, this is the *simplest* selling method of any that you will ever see, and second, this is the only one which promises you that you will have fun doing it. Let's look at these two differences.

First, I say that it is the simplest of all selling skills methods. It is simple, and it has taken me most of my training life to make it simple, and believe me, it wasn't easy to *make* it simple. Who was it who apologised for writing such a long letter because he didn't have time to write a short one? When I started sales training, I am ashamed to say, my courses were really intellectual exercises in the academic theory of salesmanship. I took money from people for doing it, too, which should have put me in jail. Over the years I have pared away, whittled down, pruned and excised until the method I use is truly the simplest you will ever find. In fact, it is so simple that the guts of selling can be stated in one sentence, and we shall be doing exactly that.

The fact that it is a simple method doesn't mean that it is crude or primitive or unrefined; on the contrary, it is subtle and delicate and perceptive. No, all I mean is that there is nothing *complicated* about selling. Selling is *simple*. Yes, it is. It really is.

Second, I say that my selling method is fun. Now, I am sure that you have been told that selling is challenging, that it can be exciting and that it is a very rewarding job, both financially and emotionally. Fine and true; it can be all those. But have you ever been told that creative selling can be a hell of a lot of *fun*? And I do truly mean just that – fun! What do *you* get fun from? Is it laying down a full house, queens on the roof, in front of your disgusted poker school and raking in the pot? Is it digging your fingers into the rock above you and pulling yourself up until there are no more rocks and you are at the summit of the mountain? Is it catching a two-iron right on the sweet-spot and watching the ball move right-to-left in a draw like a poem and just carry the bunker? That is the sort of fun that selling can be, and if you don't believe me, go and find a really successful salesman, stick this paragraph under his nose, and ask him if I lie.

All right, let's quit walking around it and kicking the tyres; let's climb in and hit the road.

10

Why does anybody ever do anything?

If we can find the answer to this all-embracing question we shall have the business of selling all wrapped up. If you want to make someone do something – and you do, you want him to buy what you sell – then first you have to find out what makes him do it. *This* is the secret of selling; not the long lists of clever 'techniques', not the hackneyed 'steps of the sale', not the tricky ways to back the customer into a corner. The true secret of selling is this, and it is simplicity itself: if you want me to do something, *find out why I do it.*

This is the direct opposite to the way that most sales training is done. Most of it says something like this: 'What has the product got that we can sell? Well, it has a titanium-plated chuffer-bearing.' All training says that you can't sell what's *in* the product, you have to sell what it *does* for the customer. Fine, so the next thing to do is ask: 'What does the titanium plating in the bearing *do*?' Some research reveals that at speeds above seven thousand rpm the bearing will stay cool, which leads to longer bearing life, which leads to a considerable saving of money and time in bearing replacements. Great! We have a benefit, an advantage, an asset, an edge on the competition, who only have a cupro-bronze chuffer bearing – let them eat their hearts out.

So, to the strains of 'See the Conquering Hero Comes' we ride out to sell the virtues of our plated bearing. Our product is mainly used in the polyploid industry and we call on polyploid factories.We see the right people, we extol the virtues of bearings that stay cool, man, even at seven thou.

We don't make a single sale.

Why not? What happened? Our product was better than the

opposition product. (Let's even say that our price was the same as theirs, too; why not make it as tough as possible?) We could *show* that ours was superior; we had these independent tests of our bearing running at well over seven thousand revs with a block of ice resting on the casing. Yet we failed to sell. Why?

We failed because we went about it the wrong way. Instead of saying: 'Why would this particular person want to buy this product?' We said: 'Here's a strong benefit which nobody else can claim, so let's go out and sell the living daylights out of it.' The fact that in the polyploid industry nobody ever runs his machines at more than four thousand revolutions per minute, at which speed the ordinary cupro-bronze bearings last for ever and a day, didn't occur to us.

Stay with me on this point for a while because it is the single most important part of all selling. In the old days before there was any sales training at all, the salesman showed his wares and said something like: 'Here's a new line of kazachoks; how do you like 'em?' The customer might say unenthusiastically: 'Yeah? What's so marvellous about them?' The salesman hadn't thought of that one. Hell, it was going to be one of those days. 'Well,' hesitantly, and then with a flash of brilliance he would say: 'Hey, it's got a built-in fluff-extractor.' And that was his sales talk.

Now, any modern selling skills practitioner would hold up his hands in disgust at this. He would say: 'NO! Don't tell him what it's made of or what it contains, tell him what it will DO!' Quite right, of course, and this is the conventional benefit idea of pretty well all the sales training taught today.

The funny thing is that while that was an example of lousy selling because it mentioned the FEATURE (what the product HAD) instead of the BENEFIT (what the product DID), many products *are* sold with the use of the feature idea only. It isn't very good selling and it makes sales trainers go into catatonic shock to hear it, but it often does work. Here's an extract from an advertisement: what picture does it produce in your mind?

'Genuine West of England, all wool upholstery; electric overdrive; burr walnut dashboard; overhead camshaft, V-12 engine; central locking system; factory-installed air-conditioning.'

Every one of those points is a *feature* – it tells how the product is made, not what it does – yet that sort of advertising sells a lot of motorcars. Why? Well, what happens is that the listener *translates* the 'what it's got' into 'what'll it do'. When you read the advertisement you automatically translated 'walnut dashboard' into 'appearance and prestige', and 'factory-installed air conditioning' into 'comfort and reliability'. If I say to you: 'This is a twelve-year-old, single malt Scotch whisky,' you automatically translate the 'it's got' into 'it'll do' in your head, and you know what the product will taste like; it will taste like an angel's kiss.

Ah, but how did you know that? You knew it from *experience*. You have had experience of that type of product before and therefore you could do your own translation. In the same way if you said to a mechanical engineer: 'This is a spur drive and this is a hypoid drive,' you need go no further; his experience with the types of gear immediately and automatically put him in the picture. He has made the jump from 'got' to 'do'. (In fact, you had damn well better *not* go any further – engineers have a short fuse when it comes to laymen trying to teach them their own business.)

So it depends on who you are talking to. Generally, while saying 'it's got this' is better than saying nothing at all, it is much stronger to say: 'it's got this, so it does that'. This is the old, tried and tested 'FEATURE-BENEFIT' idea, which is the basis of every sales training course in the world. They don't always use the words 'feature-benefit' but that's what they are saying.

Why doesn't it work better than it does? It's logical, so why isn't it more effective? It is not as good as it sounds because, as I say, it is usually applied the wrong way around. Instead of asking: 'Why should he buy?' we ask: 'What will it do for him?' Wrong way round.

One or two examples (and we can't ever practise this too often, since it is the whole cornerstone of selling):

I once met a man who, I was told, was pretty well heeled, having made a fortune on the stock market and retired before he was fifty. You wouldn't have known it by looking, since he lived in a modest little pad, drove a rusty, seven-year-old estate car, seldom travelled, and bought his clothes from factory shops. It was only when I played golf with him that I realised what turned this man on. He had the sort of equipment that you would expect to see if Liberace had taken up golf. Lord knows how many baby wallabies had died to make his golf bag; his woods were fashioned from carbon-graphite and their heads were protected with covers made from karakul skins; his irons were investment-cast from beryllium, and his golf spikes were real alligator – the man was a walking ecological disaster area.

The point? Only too simple. Try to get this man interested in a better house, newer car or tailormade business suit and you would probably fail. Show him golf tees made from the horns of the sable antelope and he would follow you through a minefield to buy them at any price.

Another one. A salesman was having no joy at all trying to sell additional truck lighting to the transport manager of a fleet of trucks. The lighting, it had been proved, was successful in cutting down accidents at night, and these trucks as it happened did a lot of night work. Fewer accidents of course meant greater safety to life and limb for the truck drivers.

The salesman pointed this out; in fact he got quite emotional about the drivers getting home safely to the bosoms of their families. None of this had the slightest effect on the transport manager. Then, quite by chance and more or less as an aside, the salesman mentioned the hassle of all the paperwork resulting from an accident. The accident reports, the insurance claims, the quotations for repair work and so on. His listener came to life. 'Hell, that's true!' he said: 'Look at this rubbish on my desk from the accident last week. Stupid driver broke his leg, too, so in addition to all the usual paper I've got hospital accounts, medical aid forms – if your lights can stop this sort of waste of time for me then maybe I'd better look into your proposition.'

Without commenting on the character of the transport manager as a warm, caring human being, this example does show the weakness of working *from* the benefit idea *to* the customer, instead of the other way around.

Never say: 'The Product has this which means it does that. Fine! Let's go and tell the customer about it.'

Always say: 'What does this person want from a product? Well, how can my product give him that?'

[93]

That's the way to go. Get into the habit of thinking this way around and you will be ahead of every salesman who is still thinking 'Feature-Benefit'.

The chink in the armour

'In days of old, when knights were bold,' as the old song had it. Not so bold, perhaps, because no self-respecting knight would have dreamt of going into battle without a lot of slabs of metal covering him from head to toe. This made it difficult for his opponents to stick it to him. If you wanted to lay him level with the gravel you had to find a weak spot. There *was* a weak spot; in order for the knight to be able to wave his arms around there had to be a joint at the shoulder, and that is what his adversaries went for. A good chop at the shoulder with a halberd and scratch one knight.

The armourers of the Middle Ages became so irritated with the number of bitterly-complaining, one-armed knights hanging around that they invented the pauldron, which was a covering over the shoulder joint. After that, if you wanted to show your dislike of a knight you had to wait until he sneezed, whereupon you stuck a pike into his unprotected throat.

In more modern times anti-tank gunners like to place their weapons so that the tank has to breast a rise, thus exposing its lightly-armoured underside.

The lightning speed of the mongoose is the only thing that stops it being bitten by the cobra during the initial skirmishing, but its speed wouldn't help it in the clinches if it caught the snake anywhere on its body except right behind the head – this is the only part where it is safe from the fangs and the venom.

Mark Twain said: 'If you want to beat a man, do it on his own subject, because he thinks he knows all about it, and he doesn't – nobody does.' If I get a poisoned finger it is usually nothing but a painful nuisance; for a professional violinist or a fashion model or a surgeon it is a potential calamity.

All of these are examples of what I call *Vulnerable Areas*, and every single human being on this planet, with the exception of saints and morons, has them. They are the weak spots, the un-protected shoulder-joints. Find mine and you *own* me.

Now, wait! Don't throw the book down in disgust, convinced that we are talking nasty here, that Machiavelli lives. Remember our definition of selling, or look it up in the dictionary. One definition is: 'Persuade to accept or approve of something.' The key word here is *persuade*. Salespeople are in the *persuasion* business, which is white-hat and nice, not the *manipulation* business, which is black-hat and grotty.

What is the difference? Essentially, it is in our attitude to the business of selling. Adolph Hitler and Winston Churchill were both in the selling business; they sold ideas to millions of people. But when Churchill said: 'I have nothing to offer but blood, toil, tears and sweat,' he was *persuading*, and doing it magnificently. When Hitler said: 'People will more easily fall victim to a big lie than to a small one,' he was demonstrating the attitude of *manipulation*, and the hell with him.

This doesn't mean that there are not salesmen who can't or don't manipulate; on the contrary, many can and do. You get unethical salesmen just as you get unethical window-cleaners, chiropodists, jockeys and ferryboat captains, and there are salespeople all over the world who sell by immorally working on the emotions of their listeners.

'Are you going to rest easy in your grave knowing that you have left your family to starve because you were too cheap to buy this extra hundred thousand of life cover?' This, said to a man who is desperately trying to make ends meet, is about as nasty as one can get. This sort of character degrades the selling business, and he helps to perpetuate the old idea of the pedlar who would sell his own mother to the white slave-traders. These are in the minority, thank heaven, but they do exist. They are not professional salesmen and they never will be. When the roll is called up yonder they won't be there.

So. We don't manipulate but we certainly do persuade. The most effective way in the world to persuade anybody of anything is to do it by way of his Vulnerable Areas (call them VA's). If we do this with a genuine desire to help the listener, instead of a genuine desire to rip him off, then go for it with a clear conscience.

What are the VA's? Again, and as usual, depends who you're talking to, but here and in no special order are some typical Vulnerable Areas. As you read through them, try to apply them to

[95]

your family, your friends, associates and business colleagues, your sporting partners and opponents. Try to find what presses their hot buttons. This is an exercise in people analysis, which is of course one of the essential skills of any salesman.

Pride

In the Pride family, and it is one of the most common of all the VA's, there are many brothers. There is Prestige, the educated one; Arrogance, the tough one; Conceit, the weak one; and Pomposity, the ridiculous one. How very simple it is to persuade Pride! What a very powerful tool a man puts in your hands when he shows that he is vulnerable in this area!

All normal people have a degree of pride in their make-up. It is listed as one of the seven deadly sins, but by itself it is not a sin. Find someone who has no pride at all and you have found a sheep, a follower of others who will never amount to very much. He can be persuaded, but not through pride. He has other VA's, but not this one.

You may be saying: 'I'm not motivated by pride, but I'm no sheep, either. This one wouldn't work on me.' No? Let me ask you – Where do you live? What's the address of your home? Ah, well, that's a good suburb. Why did you choose to buy a house just there? I see; it's convenient for the children's schools, it's not far from your club, and fairly close to the freeway so that you can get to work easily. Oh, come *on*, now; just between us buddies – it's a very nice address, isn't it? You didn't mind in the least telling me where you lived, did you now?

My job requires that I spend time in departure lounges at airports waiting for flights, and to avoid dying of boredom I tend to study my fellow man. I travel economy class because there is enough of the Cape Dutch ancestry left in me to resist paying all that extra money for three inches more seat width and a free drink. So, I get the economy boarding pass which is green and I stick it in my pocket any old way. Have a look when you are next in a departure lounge and you will see a fascinating phenomenon. All the first-class passengers – the ones with *red* passes – casually put their passes in their top pockets, and *always* with the red side showing.

Pride, prestige, conceit – we all have it in some way or other and it is a powerful persuader. Yes, you do, too; that car you drive has the mysterious and exotic initials 'GTX' on its rear. This means that it is much more expensive than the common-or-garden 'GL'. Why are the initials on the car? You presumably know which model you bought and don't need reminding, and it hardly matters to *me* what model *you* drive. Pride of possession, friend, and you know it.

Family

Do you have a family? Then you know how very vulnerable you are in anything which has to do with your loved ones. This is a very common type of persuasion and it can be either nice or nasty, depending on the thinking behind it. A man can extend himself and reach remarkable heights of achievement, simply because he wants to give his family the best of everything.

There is of course nothing against pointing out to a person the wonderful things that can happen to his loved ones if he takes a certain course of action, and very often it is only when we do talk in this way that we start a fire inside him. This would work only if he had the right feelings for his family. If he can't stand the sight of his children and never talks to his wife then you won't get out of the starting-gate.

Playtime

It is astonishing what effort a person will take, what grinding labours he will assume, what extraordinary lengths he will go to, in order to be able to sit on a rock all day holding a fishing pole and staring at nothing. Our leisure time is very important to all of us, and the salesman who shows us how to gain more of it or ensure that we have it will always get a good hearing.

Always, always, it depends who we are talking to. A lot of men count the days and hours until they can retire and do their version of nothing. But what about the person, and there are many of them, who wants nothing more than to keep sweating it out at his job? Oh, yes, he exists, and don't talk leisure time to him or you will get a blank stare. His VA lies elsewhere; find it and persuade.

Security

So far it may seem to you that the VA's we have been discussing apply only to personal selling, that is, selling to a private individual rather than to a company official. Perhaps, but as we shall see later, we *never* talk only to an official; we are always also talking to the person behind the title. Anyway, this VA applies at all levels and in all types of selling.

Man has an atavistic need for security. Ever since our prognathous ancestor rolled a rock in front of his cave to avoid being part of the diet of the sabre-toothed tiger we have been aware that we live in dangerous times. Security is always high on anyone's list of priorities. The frightened, cowering mouse is not far under the skin of the bravest of us.

It is too obvious to go into detail about the VA's of selling burglar alarms or safety doors to a home-owner. But let us not forget that when we sell to, say, the chief buyer of a company we should also be using this VA, and not only from the point of view of loss of security of the *company*. As I said, we are also talking to the man behind the title, and when he makes any decision at all he is considering two completely different aspects.

The first, presuming that he is a good company man with the interests of his employers at heart, is of course the effect the decision will have on the prosperity of the company which pays his salary. The second, and never forget it, is the eleventh commandment in business, which is: 'Thou shalt protect thine own buns at all times'. It is an interesting facet of selling that many buying decisions are made with the buyer asking himself: 'How will I come out of this? Will I be the blue-eyed boy, or will my butt be burnt to a cinder?'

Greed

I have a normal, healthy desire for the good things of life, but you – well, you are greedy. It depends who is doing the talking, doesn't it? Perhaps it would sound better if we called it acquisi-tiveness, which sounds more refined and means the same thing. Whatever we call it, it is a powerful VA. The wish to possess is common to all of us in different degrees – more for a miser, less for a hermit.

Do I have to make the point that while we *use* VA's to per-suade people, we don't *talk* about them or identify them? The salesman who told me: 'Sir, you will gain a lot of prestige from wearing this mohair suit,' was rewarded with the sight of my back as I left his emporium. I may have pride as a VA, but I don't want my nose rubbed in that fact. If he talked about the satisfaction of wearing a finely-crafted garment, thus implying that I had the good taste to appreciate such things, he might have got some-where. (In fact, he wouldn't have, since prestige is not a strong VA for me – there are other chinks in my armour, but a wish for personal status is not one of them.)

Conformity

'Do you want to be the only girl in the class who fails?' Can be a powerful weapon in persuasion, if a somewhat brutal one. It has scared the hell out of a million children, with, for all we know, beneficial results. The wish to conform – or the fear of being different – is a VA which applies at all ages and levels. The interesting thing is that if asked, most of us would indignant-ly deny that conformity influenced us at all. Hell, no – not me! I'm no sheep, I'm a free-thinker, I swim against the stream.

I read a letter to a newspaper in which the writer, a teenager, stated that he wore long hair because he was a non-conformist. You and I know that in the matter of hair, the only way that he could be a non-conformist would be to – well, what? Shave it off? Dye it green? Twist it into crazy shapes? No, there are plenty of people doing all those things. I guess there is nothing he could do with his hair to prove his contempt for conformity. The truth is that the young people of today, with their off-beat clothes, their Mohawk hairstyles and their fascinating variations of the lan-guage of Shakespeare, E. M. Forster and the New Testament, are more rigidly conformist than the closest order of nuns.

[99]

Ambition

Now, this VA has always intrigued me. As we saw in the last VA, ask anyone if he is a conformist and he will probably deny it, whether he is or not. But ask anyone if he is ambitious, and he will affirm it – *whether he is or not*. We have managed to arrange things so that our herd philosophy makes it a sort of a crime not to be ambitious. We are afraid to say: 'No. I have found my place in life. I fill that place with competence and personal dignity and even grace. I have no ambition.' You will never ever hear anyone say anything like those words, and isn't it a pity?

The truth, of course, is that everyone is indeed ambitious, but when we ask a job applicant whether or not he is ambitious we mean, does he intend to hitch his wagon to a star? We are all ambitious for something, but while Horace wants to be the President of the company, Charlie wants to be the President of the company bowling team.

Either way, ambition is a VA. It isn't necessarily the grievous fault that Mark Antony pretended to condemn, but it drives men to tremendous effort, and it can be used as an effective persuader if the right button is pressed.

Enough; you should be able to extend this short list of VA's with a little thought, based on your own experience of your fellow-man. The point is that we are *all* vulnerable in some way or another, and the creative salesman uses these vulnerabilities in order to persuade.

Again, may I beg you to lose any idea you may have that this is somehow unethical or immoral; it is, only if your attitude makes it so. If you genuinely wish to help, if you know for certain that the product, plan, service or idea will improve things for him in some way or another, then the only way to get past the armour of apathy, indifference or ignorance is to find the chink, the weak spot, the soft under-belly.

Think back to some of the purchases you have made because a salesman found a VA in you. If you would like to find that salesman and make him eat the product you bought then he used the VA maliciously or cynically. If on the other hand you would like to shake his hand and thank him then he used the VA honestly and ethically – and he showed himself to be a creative salesman.

Why people do things

Discard all the decoration, dispense with all the verbiage, cut away all the undergrowth, and we find that people do things for two reasons and two reasons only: to achieve a GAIN or avoid a LOSS. There are no other reasons for taking any action, there never have been and there never will be. Everything that anyone has ever done from Moses climbing the mountain to Armstrong stepping on to the moon was done in order to get something or to avoid losing something.

You know this already, don't you? So why make such a big thing about it? Because we forget it, and if we are to be creative salesmen we can't afford to forget it.

Perhaps you don't entirely believe this great truth. Perhaps you feel that it is too simplistic, that man is such a highly complex entity that there must be something far more involved or esoteric behind the motivation for taking action. Let us examine one or two examples to try to prove that any action, no matter how subtle or intricate, has its roots in the GAIN-LOSS idea.

For openers I suppose that the story of the Good Samaritan will do as well as any. In this, the first recorded case of mugging, we have on the face of it two villains and one hero. What made the priest and the Levite pass by? What made the Samaritan stop? Gain and loss, of course; nothing else. Let us assume the best motives for the priest. He would have liked to stop and help. But he was on his way to give an important sermon to a group of sinners, and this was just one man. Instead of saving one body, he was going to save fifty souls! He was no doubt able to give himself this acceptable reason for his action – the gain was greater than the loss, and he passed by on the other side.

The Levite was a compassionate man and he would have liked to stop and help. But he had heard of these tricks on the Jericho road where a man lies naked and apparently wounded. Go across to help him and his fellow thieves jump out of the culvert and beat you to a pulp. The Levite had a fat purse, too; he had worked hard for the money, and he could not jeopardise his family's future, what with inflation taking the cream off his profits. No way; the fear of loss was greater than the wish to gain, and he resisted the temptation to help and passed by on the other side.

[101]

Those two are fairly simple, but what about the Samaritan? What did he gain by giving the casualty first-aid, allowing him to use his transport and paying for his accommodation at the motel? Was it the warm glow we get from doing a good deed, the satisfaction of doing something which others were not prepared to do, the feeling that the recording angel nodded in approval and put a big tick on the credit side of the ledger? Maybe; we shall never know. The point is that in this case, as in all others, the doer of the deed, the taker of the action, *actually had no choice*. The Samaritan balanced the Gain/Loss concept in his mind and he did what he did because he had to do it.

I am close to a group of people, most of them young, who belong to an organisation which fights organised and in most cases legalised cruelty to animals. In particular, they oppose the slaughter of fur-bearing animals and the painful use of animals in the cosmetic industry. They don't enjoy it, God knows; they are faced with the most horrific details of systematic cruelty. They fight an unequal struggle with the billion-dollar cosmetic houses and the fur trade, and they battle against ignorance, apathy, cynicism and greed.

Why do they do it? Well, they are afflicted with compassion, which is an uncomfortable VA to have, but when you really get down to it you find that they use their time and effort and money *because they have no choice*. They cannot pass by on the other side.

We do many things because if we did not do them we could not look in the mirror in the morning. The loss of self-respect would be too much.

You carry wherever you go a balance-scale in your head. The question: 'Should I do this? Should I take this action?' is answered very simply by putting the gain or loss in one side or other of the scale. You do this automatically; you can't help doing it and you don't even know you are doing it. Anything which requires a decision – selling your house, taking up croquet, stopping smoking (or starting a career in selling) – you do these things or don't do them by seeing which side of the scale is heavier.

And the scale swings one way or the other because of one thing only – your Vulnerable Areas.

*   *   *

[102]

Now, wasn't that a crazy way to start to look at the business of selling? Where are the usual 'Steps of the sale'? What about all the clever gimmicks? Why no long lists of techniques?

We are doing it the right way around, remember? Instead of: 'The product has this, therefore it does that for the customer' we are asking ourselves: 'What would make him want it? Why does he buy things?'

That's the way to go.

COFFEE-BREAK 2: HOW TO BEAT THE HELL OUT OF COMPETITION

This is the name of the selling game, isn't it? We would all like to be able to beat the ears off that bunch of roughnecks across the street. If we had the secret of crushing competition how pleasant our job would be! We would make our calls and take our orders, confident that when any opposition salesman dared to try to flog his trashy wares around our bailiwick we had the ammunition to sit back and blow him out of the water. Life would be a ball.

Well, there *is* a way to beat the hell out of opposition. It is ignored or neglected by most salesmen because it isn't very exciting or dramatic or sensational. It isn't infallible, it isn't magical, but in the long haul it is the only way to make sure that when you are up against really tough competition, you are able to give it your very best shot.

There are three ways which I have seen salesmen use against competition; they are The Ostrich Attitude, The Mafioso Solution, and The Gladiator Concept. This is how they work:

The Ostrich Attitude

The protagonists of this method say: 'If we all put our heads in the sand and keep perfectly quiet, perhaps the opposition will go away and quit bothering us.' It may be hard to believe, but there are many companies who operate by closing their eyes and ears to anything to do with opposition products, apparently under the impression that if they ignore the enemy it will fold its tents and disappear. I get salesmen telling me: 'Opposition doesn't bother me – as far as I'm concerned it just doesn't exist!' Whether or not this character expects me to burst into applause or award him a Nobel Prize I really don't know, but my reaction to that valiant-sounding piece of nonsense is that the salesman must be half-witted.

When a salesman claims that he is the golden boy, that his products are perfect and that his opposition are a bunch of losers selling a lot of rubbish, it may seem that he is a true positive thinker with the right attitude. In fact nothing could be more wrong. He does not have the right attitude. What he is engaged in is not positive thinking, but living in a dream world. The opposition most surely *is* out there, it *does* exist, it *is* getting its share of the market – and the longer a salesman ignores it the more chance he is giving it to grab some of *his* share of that market.

The Ostrich Attitude does not work. Stick your head in the sand and before you know it the opposition will be pulling out your tail-feathers and selling them to your customers.

The Mafioso Solution

The second way of handling opposition is beautiful in its simplicity; when they bug you, you send around a couple of guys in black shirts and two-tone shoes to break their arms and legs. Well, not literally, of course. I call this method the Mafioso Solution because it consists of *knocking* the opposition, not physically but verbally. There are different versions of the Solution – here is the Sawn-off Shotgun Approach:

> 'Are you really going to use their epoxy resin? Do you want to get dermatitis clear up to your armpits?'
> 'I have it from the horse's mouth that the company is going broke, so if you buy their word-processors you will cry like a baby when you need parts and service.'

Then there is the indirect, or Mafia Kiss Effect:

> 'For a small, new company with no facilities or experience, I think they are to be commended for their courage.'

'I don't say that their advertising is actually misleading, but by golly, it is very, very *clever*.'

Either way, The Mafioso Solution seeks to beat opposition by knocking it, by running it down, derogating it and generally telling customers that it is overpriced, unsafe, tacky, useless and in every way the prize lemon of the year.

Every sales course, every book or film on selling deplores the custom of knocking the opposition, on the grounds that it is *unethical*. My own angle on this is far more simple than any venture into the mystique of ethics; as far as I am concerned knocking is unacceptable simply because it is second-rate selling. If the only way you can sell me your product is to tell me how lousy the other product is then you brand yourself a mediocre salesman. The salesman who says or implies: 'Well, maybe my product isn't perfect, but it's a lot better than that other junk,' will never be a pro because that is not the way of the pro.

Oddly enough, and I hate to admit this, there is a weird sort of customer who likes to hear a salesman badmouthing the other fellow's products. You will hear him say: 'Wow, that guy certainly showed up the opposition stuff for the rubbish it is!' I have very little to say to this character, and I have never been able to sell to him. He is a sucker for the slick talker and the high-pressure artist, and he makes some very unfortunate purchases. Luckily he is in a minority; most buyers resent a salesman who knocks others, and they accord him very little of their time and even less of their respect.

The Gladiator Concept

When the ancient Romans borrowed from the Etruscans the idea of men fighting to the death in hand-to-hand combat, their fighters were recruited from the ranks of criminals and slaves. The best among them – the pro's – eventually became folk heroes and cult figures. Next to the name of a gladiator carved on a wall in Pompeii is scratched: 'The maiden's delight!'

There is a close similarity between the ancient gladiator and the modern salesman. They both fight it out in single combat. If the salesman doesn't win, he doesn't eat; if the gladiator didn't win, he didn't live. They use different weapons from those of their antagonists. The salesman is selling his electrical grinders against his opponent's pneumatic grinders, while the Roman who fought with a shield and a sword fought a man who used a net and a trident.

The best of the old fighters were good because they knew exactly what the opposition was able to do. The *gladiator* (which simply means 'swordsman') knew to the inch how far the *retiarius* could reach with his trident and how best to dodge the deadly net which he threw. The retiarius knew that if he allowed the gladiator to get in close with that short stabbing sword he was dogmeat. They knew the strong and weak points of each other's weapons and they knew how to counter the strong points and to exploit the weak ones.

The key word in that last paragraph, repeated over and over again, is *knew*. They *knew* their own weapons and they were adept in their use. They *knew* their enemy's weapons and how to meet their threat.

This is the way to beat the hell out of the opposition. The way is through in-depth *knowledge*, and there is no other. I said that salesmen tend to bypass or ignore this way. They find it much more exciting to ride out to battle instead of first doing the painstaking research on products and their application to the customer's needs, on opposition products, the strong points and the weak points. Not in order to knock them but to *know* them, backwards, forwards, sideways and up and down.

If you have never sold anything before, then this is the best advice I can ever give you; it is the best advice you will ever hear about becoming a creative salesman:

Know your products. Know everything about them. Know your opposition products. Learn as much as you can about them. You will not fall into the error of getting so involved in the opposition that you forget what you are selling, nor will you ever know as much about the opposition as you do about your own company, products, policies and procedures; that is to be expected. But the more you *know*, the more confidence you will have; the more you *know*, the less you *fear*.

Promise you.

[107]

11

The narrowing of choice

Here's a way to look at a salesman's job which you may not have thought of. Consider the situation: the salesman has a *product* and he has a *prospect*, and his job is to bring these two together. Is that not a reasonable definition? All right, how does he do this?

Before the salesman has talked to the prospect, what is in the prospect's mind? He could have several thoughts wandering around in his head. As you realise by now, since the most important thing for a salesman's success is what goes on in the head of the prospect, we are spending some time in there. Here are some examples:

I urgently need to buy something. I know just what it is, who sells it, how much it costs and how it works. I shall get in touch with the salesman right now.

I do need to buy something. I know more or less what I want, but not the actual brand. I have an idea of the price range and roughly how the product works. I'll get around to calling some companies pretty soon.

I might need to buy something sometime. I don't know how it works, what it costs or who sells it.

I have no idea of buying anything. Why should I? I don't need anything, now or in the foreseeable future.

I am definitely not going to buy anything.

Somewhere between the first and the last thought is where we will find our prospects. The first one is red-hot, the last is ice-cold. Now, we know our prospect. How well we know him depends on how much research we have been able to do. We might know him very well indeed or we might only have started to compile a dossier on him. Either way, we have a good idea of what he needs, and we shall be finding out more about him with each word he says in our interview.

If we take the first thought above as applying to him then of course our work has largely been done already, always assuming that the product he is about to buy is ours and not the opposition's. But suppose that what is going on in his mind is thought number four? 'I have no idea of buying anything. Why should I? I don't need anything, now or in the foreseeable future.'

There's a tough one! How on earth are we going to sell to a man who hasn't the slightest idea of buying? If we were to use the old Feature-Benefit idea we would jump in with our product and hit him with some 'It's got, therefore it'll do' techniques to try to make him excited about buying. It probably won't work and we know why not; that is the wrong way to go about it. If we approach it from the prospect's angle instead of the product's virtues, we can move him from this thought:

'I have no choice to *make*.'

To this one:

'I have no other *choice*.'

I call this method 'The Narrowing of Choice', and that is precisely what it is – a narrowing down or lessening of the original wide field of thoughts in his mind to a one-way path where he buys because he has no choice. He has no choice, not because you won't give him one but because his own logical thinking has made him realise that he has one path to tread, and only one.

Our example is Horace, the office manager of the Transverse Ovoid Manufacturing Company, a medium-sized business, solid, conservative, consolidation-minded. Our product is an office copier. It is slightly higher than the average price but not so much that it should scare anyone. We know that Horace is against these gimmicky, new-fangled gadgets, which should tell us a good deal about him right there. Some years ago he fought to the death the idea of changing over to electric typewriters, and there is a standing offer of the George Cross to the first salesman to approach him with a word-processor. His senior management leaves Horace to make his own decisions because apart from his old-fashioned ideas he is a very good man; loyal to the company, hard-working, fair to his staff.

We have no trouble making an appointment to see Horace because our research has told us that his really busy time is towards the twenty-fifth of the month when all hell breaks loose. This is when the monthly figures must go out, and the office staff is flat out.

1. To buy or not to buy?

The first thing to ask ourselves is: What is he doing now which we want him to change? The answer is that he is doing without copying machines and his poor typists are running themselves ragged every month-end to try to cope with the load of work. We have to show him the urgency of making a decision NOW.

'It must be a real problem for you at the end of the month to make sure that the sales figures go out on time, without putting too much of a burden on your staff.' The average salesman talks about the *product*; the pro salesman talks about the *problem*. You can write that in letters of fire. The customer isn't interested in the product, he wants the problem taken off his back. We have tried to use a VA here by talking about his staff; what we know about Horace indicates that he is well-disposed towards his people and aware of the heavy work-load at month-end. Our question is therefore aimed at moving Horace from: 'I have no idea of buying anything. Why should I? I don't need anything,' to 'Hey! Maybe there is something, somewhere, which could help me.'

[110]

2. Broad Need Area

What *sort* of product would help overcome the overload? 'Other busy managers have found that since most of the work of a typing pool is copy-typing, it makes sense to have a fast, low-cost machine do the work instead of using a highly-trained typist.' The salesman is keeping the need area very broad at this stage; he is talking the general idea of copying machines and staying a mile away from any mention of his own machine. The last thing he wants is to talk brand names yet.

'Also, you have probably found that the best typists dislike the drudgery of copy-typing, and prefer to do more creative work.' Here's his VA again; he is an industrious person, we know that already, so we don't bear down on anything which will mean less work for him. If, however, we can show him how his staff can be used for more useful and more interesting work then maybe we have something for him.

All right, time to do some more narrowing:

3. Specific Need Areas

What *type* of copier would do the job best? 'A photo-copier, needing no special maintenance and which would be simplicity to use, would be popular with your girls and they would not be afraid to use it.' There are different types of copier on the market – electrostatic types, types which use special paper sensitive to heat, straight photographic ones, and so on. Now is the time to narrow the choice down to one *type*; not your brand yet, but the type which your brand fits into.

4. Good news gained

Now's the time to narrow it down to your product, by showing the specific results which meet his specific needs. 'From looking at your situation it seems that the WOW Model 1000 would do exactly what you want a copier to do. Your sales figures would go out on time, the sales department would be happy, and your team would not have to look forward with dread to the coming of the twenty-fifth of the month.'

5.   Bad news avoided

'Yes, it's quite true that some of your staff are against the idea of a copier, but we found that they were worried about having to replace chemicals and powder in the machine. The WOW 1000 has nothing to replace, no maintenance necessary and no messy chemicals. Perhaps you yourself have had the experience of a company buying the wrong type of machine and because the office staff were unhappy about using it, it gathered dust in the store-room. We find that the WOW 1000 is one of the most popular copiers on the market because people don't fear to use it.'

You are not knocking any one particular make of copier, but there is absolutely nothing wrong with showing the actual and factual shortcomings of a certain *policy of manufacture* – and that is what is happening here.

6.   Preferred supplier

This stage may not be necessary if you are the only place where he can get the WOW 1000, but it does happen that you sell a product which he can buy from another source of supply. Since it is no great fun to sell a person on a product and then have him buy it from someone else, you have to narrow his choice even more. Now that he has decided that the only copier which will satisfy his needs is the WOW 1000, you have to show him that the only place in the world to buy the WOW 1000 is your company. 'No matter how good a product is, you will appreciate that it has to be properly serviced and also covered by the best guarantee in the business. We believe that as the agents with the longest experi-ence of handling the WOW 1000 we are in the best position to look after our machines and our customers.' *That* should tie him up nice and tight.

What you have just read is not a sales talk. We shall be looking at one or two sales talks later on and we'll have some fun with them. This is merely to show what the real job of a salesman is all about. We have to move the prospect from: 'I don't need to buy anything,' through 'If I did buy anything it wouldn't be now,' through 'If I did buy anything now it wouldn't be a falderal,' through 'If by any chance at all I decided to buy a falderal, it wouldn't be a *diagonal* falderal,' through 'And if I bought a diagonal falderal it probably wouldn't be from *you*,' all the way to 'Where do I sign?'

That's it, you see; we narrow his choice. We do it not with gimmicks or smart-talking him but by using his VA's and tying them up with how our product will meet them.

It is one of the most interesting phenomena in selling, to watch a man realise first, that he has a need; second, that the need is now; third, that the need can be filled by a product; fourth, that it has to be a specific product; fifth, that there is one source for that product.

I promised you fun, didn't I? That's fun!

12

'How much is it?'

We are about to discuss the question of price.

Before we say another word on this subject, let us understand that this is to some salesmen one of the most fearsome things in the whole selling business. Whenever they realise that the product they are selling is a little higher-priced than the opposition they go into shock and they are unable to make even a halfway decent sales presentation. They fear the time when the listener grunts, scratches his nose and says: 'Yeah, I see what the product's all about. Tell me – how much it it?'

Faced with this horrifying question the salesman now has two options. He can duck the question by putting off the answer for as long as possible, until the impatient listener says: 'Come on, come on – what's it cost?' Or he can come out flat-footed and tell him the price. Whereupon he is certain that the listener will fall down dead.

For most of my time as a field salesman I sold products or services which were higher in price than the opposition, and I had my full share of interesting reactions to my higher price. Since you will certainly be getting some resistance to your product on the price side (there is *always* a cheaper product than yours around somewhere, so you will always get a price resistance from someone), you might like to see in advance the sort of thing you can expect. Here is a selection from my notes in the field:

- 'You must be joking!'

- 'What are you selling these days – the Crown Jewels?'

- 'Your opposition is about *half* that!'
- 'Where did you park your Rolls-Royce?'
- 'You must be joking!'
- 'I asked for the price of one, not a dozen.'
- 'At that price, why don't you carry a gun and wear a mask?'
- 'I don't want to buy your company, thanks.'
- 'You must be joking!'

And so on. Most of these remarks were accompanied by rolling of the eyes, clutching the heart, holding up the hands to ward off the blows – my customers could have made a good living on the stage.

Now, although in my early days in selling I was also afflicted with terror at telling my prospect that my product was higher in price than the opposition, I really don't know why this should have been. I had almost every reaction in the book to my higher price, but in no single case was I offered physical violence. Nobody tried to hit me, shoot me or hang me. Nobody picked me up and threw me out of his office, factory or home. I changed my ideas about selling higher-priced products when I realised that selling them isn't *dangerous*.

I am not being flippant here. I have seen too many salesmen who are literally scared out of their socks at the prospect of talking about their higher price, and I mean really frightened. There is a real and logical reason for this fear, and it is far more serious than the fear itself. Follow me like a shadow here, because if you sell a higher-priced product and if you ever have the slightest fear, worry or apprehension about the price then this applies directly to you. Here it is:

A salesman fears the price of his product *when he himself believes that it is too high*.

There it is. If I am saying in my heart: 'My product is over-priced,' than it doesn't much matter that I am saying with my mouth: 'This is great value for money!' The customer will hear

[115]

what my heart is saying, not my mouth. As it happens, I am not a very good liar, but I don't think that anyone can successfully sell a product in which they have no faith – not in the long term, anyhow. When you believe that your product is unrealistically-priced, you have no faith in it.

How about that? Have I solved one problem for you, only to give you another, more serious one? All right, you say; so the customer can't be fooled for very long if you don't believe in the worth of the product. Where does this leave me, if I honestly think that my price is too high? What do I do – jump off the top of the office block?

Let's talk about it. Not only the price problem but the whole *shtick* of Product Confidence. If you are unhappy about the price of your product then you lack confidence, not only in the product itself but also in the pricing policy and therefore the whole marketing strategy of your company.

What do you do if you believe that your products are not as good a buy as the opposition, for whatever reason? Well, you can go to your management with your reasons, you can keep quiet about it except to your fellow salesmen and, probably, your long-suffering spouse, or you can simply resign from the company and find some greener grass on the other side of the fence.

There is one more option, and it's just as well that there *is* one more, since none of the above alternatives are very stimulating or potentially fruitful: you can examine exactly *why* you believe that the opposition is better. That sounds more like the action of a professional.

First it is necessary to recognise something. There is not one single selling organisation in the world where the entire product range is superior (or even equal) to the entire product range of every other selling organisation in that industry. I know that there are some pie-in-the-sky salespeople out there who will call me a liar but it's true.

Therefore sometimes a salesman has to say something like this: 'I have faith in my product range; taken as a whole, I sell a damn good line of products. Now sure, there are some very good companies in the same line of business as I am and they don't sell junk. It may well be true that some of their line has some very strong sales points which for certain applications I can't match. I believe that over the whole range I'm in a very strong position,

[116]

though, and this allows me to sell the whole range with confidence. I do not, therefore, pick out only those products which have no real opposition, but sell right across the range, because I know that the customer buying my whole range is getting a hell of a good line of products.' That may sound a bit pompous and of course we don't stand on the street corner and proclaim it as our philosophy; nevertheless that's the way the pro salesman thinks.

All very well, Beer, but don't duck the problem. Here is my main product line and the main product line of the opposition. As you can clearly see, they are superior to us, either in quality of manufacture, price, or any one of the many things that go with the sale of anything.

Maybe, maybe not. The only way to discover which is to go really deeply into each product, its application, its strong and weak points, its price, the back-up which the company gives, everything like that. For instance, the quality of your opposition may be superior to yours. Although their price is a little higher it is a very much better article.

Really, now? Who says so? As a field salesman I had a job once where I had to make around twenty-five calls a day. Just getting in and out of a car twenty-five times a day can turn a perfectly good suit into a rag, and when it happens to be the height of summer – well, believe me, in summer a salesman sweats. This means that one's suits spend a lot of time at the cleaners, which also doesn't do them much good.

I got tired of buying expensive suits and I voiced my annoyance to the menswear store-owner I patronised. 'Well,' he said, 'it's your own fault. You are buying too up-market. Here is a perfectly good summer-weight suit. It isn't pure wool like the ones you usually buy, but it's a hardwearing mixture and it will last just as long as the more expensive one. Also, at this price you can afford to buy two instead of one, so you give the suits a longer rest between wearings. Trust me; it's a better deal.'

It was, too. In that situation the quality product was actually *inferior* to the cheaper product! Before you complain about the opposition's better quality, look at the *application* of the product, and realise that often an apparently lower-quality product has been deliberately and carefully designed to fit neatly into a certain slot of price and application. They don't put emeralds into costume jewellery.

So. Before we scream that the opposition is slaughtering us with better products, before we turn mother's picture to the wall and simply give up, let's look at *every* aspect of our product compared with what else is available on the market. There may be the best reason in the world why our zipper is plastic while theirs is metal, our duvet is stuffed with acrylic compared with their belly-feathers of the white-faced barnacle goose, our bread is ninety-seven cents while theirs is seventy-nine cents.

Which brings us back to price.

We shall now look at a scenario which shows once and for all why so many sales presentations fail. You see, the virgin salesman who has been through his first sales course comes out of it as though he is ready to take on the PLO single-handed. He has heard the course leader talk about the steps of the sale and they make sense to him; he has practised the techniques with the sexy names and they excite him (when gaining the prospect's attention, how can you fail with a technique called 'The Karate Chop'?). He has all his sales kits, samples, brochures and his brand-new order-book; he is raring to go.

He walks into the prospect's place of business and starts his sales talk. He knows that the product is something which the prospect uses in his office or factory. He knows that he is talking to the right person, the one who can say 'Yes'. He knows that he has a good product. Here goes! And without mucking about he shows the prospect a sample of the product and begins declaiming its strong points. We enter at this point.

Salesman: One of the things we are really proud of is the design of the counterweight. As you can see –

Prospect: Whoa! Slow down, boy. What's this thing cost?

Salesman (The sales course warned against introducing the price too soon): Ah, well, all in good time, sir. Now –

Prospect: Now's as good a time as any, buddy. What's the price?

Salesman (A little flustered; they didn't mention this in the course): Uh – well, we will come to the price soon. Before we do that, I'd like to –

Prospect: We have come to the price right now. *How much*?

Salesman: Er – two hundred and ten.

Prospect (Rolling his eyes, clutching at his heart, holding up his hands to ward off the blow): You must be joking!

Right there the sales presentation dies in its tracks. It dies because the customer has taken over the talk; from now on *he* will be running the interview. It will go on until he gets tired of it, whereupon he will throw the salesman out and, smiling grimly, cut another notch in his gun. The salesman is likely to grab *his* gun and go in search of the sales trainer, who didn't tell him what it was like out there in the real world.

What do you do when the prospect complains about the price? This is one of the biggest questions in the whole selling business, and sales trainers have been trying to answer it for decades. I have probably spent as long working on the price situation as anybody, and the longer I spend on it, the simpler it seems to become. No, I did not say 'easier'. I said 'simpler', and there is a world of difference between those two words.

Way back I said that the selling process was a simple thing, that people buy for simple reasons. I made quite a point of this and you may have wondered why I went on and on about it; we have now come to the reason. I said that selling is *simple*, but nowhere back there did I say that selling was *easy*. Selling – and I mean creative selling, not merely picking orders off a hook – means changing a man's thinking, and there has never been anything easy about that. Any man who tells you that selling is easy has never cried his tears out there; but any man who tells you that selling is a complicated business is conning you.

We are now going to apply this concept to the price situation; it won't be easy, but it will be simple.

When someone complains that a product requires an unduly high outlay of capital, how does he do it? I mean by that, what are the actual words he uses? Usually you will find that he says something like this:

- 'That price is exorbitant.'
- 'No way am I going to pay that price.'

[119]

- 'Sure, it's a good product, but not at that price.'
- 'Where did you get your crazy price from?'

That's the sort of thing we hear, isn't it? Right. Now, you see something significant about those actual words, don't you? Interesting, isn't it, how the word 'price' keeps coming in all the time. The dictionary defines the word 'price' as: *the sum in money for which goods may be bought or sold.*

And that, my masters, is the root of the problem. Your prospect is complaining about the amount of money it will take him to *buy* the product, and that should not be concerning him at all.

'Of course it should be concerning him!' you could be saying. 'Hell, that's what it's all about, isn't it?'

No, and that is the whole point. I will put on this piece of paper twelve words. The whole price problem is that when the prospect says: 'That price is too high,' he is paraphrasing *the first six words.* We have got to get him thinking *the last six words.* It is as simple as they. Not easy, but simple. I promise you that if you can stop him thinking the first six words and get him thinking the last six then your price problem with that particular prospect is over. In fact, that prospect will no longer be a prospect – he will be a customer.

Here we go; we shall look at the present situation first and then at the final objective. When he complains about price:

He is thinking PRICE.
We must get him thinking COST.

He is thinking INITIAL PRICE.
We must get him thinking TOTAL COST.

He is thinking INITIAL PRICE OF BUYING THE PRODUCT.
We must get him thinking TOTAL COST OF DOING THE JOB.

There they are, just twelve words; the most important words in the whole business of selling against lower price. Let us put them opposite each other so that we can see exactly what the situation is now and what we have to change it to in the future:

INITIAL	TOTAL
PRICE	COST
OF	OF
BUYING	DOING
THE	THE
PRODUCT	JOB

I bet you are disappointed. What a let-down after all that big build-up! From what Beer said, these were going to be magic words which would overcome all our price problems, and it turns out to be gibberish.

Well, I didn't say that they would overcome all your price problems. I said that *if* – and it is a big if, certainly – *if* you can stop him thinking the left side and get him thinking the right side, he would stop yelling 'price' at you and start thinking along the lines which could bring him over to you. Also, while there is nothing magical in selling, these twelve words are the nearest you and I will ever see to a magical effect. One salesman who attended a training clinic of mine and went out and used this idea told me, and he had an awed expression on his face: 'I tell you, Michael, it was like waving a wand.'

Come on, let us see just what goes on when these twelve words work for you.

He says: 'That price is too high.' Now, that is *exactly* how his mind is working; it is working on the PRICE, and remember our dictionary definition: *the sum of money for which goods may be bought.* You see, he is thinking of how much he would have to plunk down in order, and this is the point, to *own* the product.

BUT YOU DON'T BUY THINGS TO *OWN* THEM – YOU BUY THINGS TO *USE* THEM!

You don't buy a tube of glue to own it; you buy it to use it. You don't buy a grinding wheel or an airline ticket or a diary or a foot-bath or a helicopter to own them; they are bought with the sole purpose of using them. Therefore the only thing that matters is: What does it cost to use these things? I am considering buying this bulldozer or this parachute or this nail-file in order to do a specific job with it. I am not considering these things in order to put them on my mantel-piece and admire them; they are going to be *used*.

Therefore, while the initial price is not meaningless, it is only one part of the deal – and as it happens, it is the smaller part. The larger part is the cost of doing the job once I have paid the initial price.

To look at some of these 'jobs' which we have been talking about:

- The 'job' of a bulldozer is to move a certain amount of earth over a certain number of working hours at a certain cost per cubic yard – that is why a bulldozer is bought.

- The 'job' of a parachute is to save a life by operating completely reliably on demand, to be easy to pack, to take up the smallest possible space and to resist extremes of climate and temperature – that is why a parachute is bought.

- The 'job' of a nail-file is to file excess nail-ends quickly and cleanly, to stay rust-free and sharp over a good period of time, to be convenient to stow away in a handbag and to be ready for use whenever it is needed – that is why a nail-file is bought.

I apologise for these apparently childish examples, but it is not easy to think 'cost of doing the job' when for all these years we have been thinking 'price of buying the product'.

I haven't ever done it, but some of my delegates to sales clinics have reported back that they regularly use the twelve words right there in front of the prospect, and show him on paper the difference between the left side and the right side. If you like the idea of doing this, be my guest.

Are you happy about the idea that everything is bought not to own it but to use it? Sure? Then you haven't thought it through. There are things we buy to own, with no thought of ever using them. That Lalique horse you bought your wife; after she had hugged you and kissed you, what did she do with it? Why, she put it on the mantel-piece! She isn't ever going to *use* that fragile piece of glass for anything; it was bought to be *owned*. So yes;

there are products which are not bought in order to do a job. (It could be said that the job that diamond ear-rings and silk scarves and garden gnomes do is to be admired, and while in a sense this is true it is sophistry or quibbling, and does not help our point here.) But of course these things are pure luxuries, are they not? And when you buy luxuries you approach the whole idea of price in a totally different way.

We can dispose of this apparent anomaly very quickly: you have probably heard of the Cubic Zirconium, that sneaky mineral which looks to us laymen pretty much the same as a diamond but is only a small fraction of the price. Put one of those on your sweetheart's finger and who will know? Now why don't they sell many, many more of the Cubic Zirconiums than they do? Because when it comes to luxuries such as high-class jewellery, price is a completely different concept from what it is when considering word processors and food processors.

The fact is of course that in the luxury or 'pleasure' buying business, price often stands on its head, and things are rejected for the crazy reason that they don't cost enough!

Use the twelve words. You have realised by now that they are not simply words; they are a different way of looking at a basic aspect of the selling process. Use them. Practise using them with your own product range, until you can use them confidently and skilfully.

You will be astonished at how they work for you.

13

Another look at price

Every salesman who sells higher price against lower price must eventually sit down, shake his head, and say, even if only to himself: 'Why doesn't management cut the price just a bit? Life would be so much easier!' I know that I said this more than once, especially after a tough day where everyone seemed to be throwing my price in my face.

It is all very well to be confident about the price situation when writing a book about it or when talking about it in a conference room; there are no ugly customers there. But no matter how positive a presence we exhibit, people are going to hit us with price and the most positive and confident of us are going to feel down every now and then. That is when we sit in that motel, chuck the order-book across the room and growl or snarl or whimper: 'If they would only sharpen their pencils just a little bit!' Heck, it's only human to feel that way occasionally; the best salesmen in the world have their down periods.

I don't know whether or not you realise this but the fact is that your company could make your products cheaper than they are now. Perhaps you have thought of this, but have you thought that they could do this *and that the products would be nearly as good as they are now*?

There are many ways to cut corners in manufacturing costs, so that there is really very little difference between the better one and the worse one; no matter what the product, it can be done.

Well, why the hell don't they go ahead and do it, then? They don't do it because they are not half-witted, that's why. A brief scenario:

Another look at price

Let us say that I am the boss-man of your cheaper opposition product. I know that my product is not quite as good as yours but because there will always be a market for products of different prices I have a reasonable slice of the cake and I am content. Suppose I woke up one morning and found that your company had cut its prices and that they were now competitive with mine. You have cut a few goodies off your product – not many, and not blatantly, but enough to bring down the price to where you are in the same range as me.

What am I going to do? Well, you don't think that I am going to let you get away with this, do you? No way; *I am going to cut my price again*, so that I am once again cheaper than you.

Where are you now? You are in deep trouble, that's where. If you are thinking of cutting your price again, forget it. You cannot follow me down that road because that will surely lead to disaster. Price-cutting is my *business*. I wrote the words and music of cheaper, cheaper, cheaper. Where a company stands in the price range – low, medium or high price – depends on the marketing strategy and philosophy of that company, and it is something which was decided a long time ago. History tells us that in almost every case where a marketing organisation has tried to move out of the price range where it made its name originally, either to sell cheaper than usual or to go up the scale, it has failed. There are exceptions, but they are rare.

So. You have cut your price, only to see me cut mine as well. You have gained nothing, but you have lost much. You have no price advantage or even parity, but what is far worse is that your customers, the ones who bought happily from you in spite of the higher price, have lost some of their confidence in you and your products. Your products – remember? – are not quite as good as they were. The finish is not quite so good, the quality control not quite so strict, the service not quite so prompt and expert, the back-up not quite so competent as before.

And of course, while it is so easy to drop a little in product quality, it is a long and rocky road back up again. Many companies, having lowered their standards to meet competition and found that it hasn't worked, have failed to make it up the hill again.

Your price is higher than the opposition? There are many things you can try, but whatever you do, don't move out of your

[125]

chosen price field. If you do you will be fighting the opposition *on their own ground*, on terrain which is familiar to them and strange to you, and every battle commander from Xerxes to Patton would laugh a strategy like that to scorn.

None of this means that any marketing company can sit in its ivory tower and ignore the realities of pricing to suit the changing attitudes and economic climate of the day. Clearly, pricing as a major part of the marketing mix is something which any organis- ation keeps a close and watchful eye on. But that is a far cry from desperately chasing the opposition down a Cresta Run of price- cutting. And if you think that perhaps just a teensy-weensy cut wouldn't hurt, well, it's like being a teensy-weensy bit pregnant – there's no such thing.

A last thought on price

I have sometimes said to my groups of salesmen on sales training clinics: 'If your only problem in selling is that your price is higher than the opposition, then be happy.' This once led a delegate who had recently been told by his sales manager that his product range had just had an overall price rise of twelve per cent, to remark sarcastically: 'According to Michael Beer, I must be the happiest salesman in the world.'

Nevertheless, and while my comment may be a shade over- simplified, it is fundamentally true. If you have no real problem with your product range except higher prices than the crowd over the road, then offer up a prayer to whatever gods protect you. I have worked with salesmen who have no price problems at all; they have others, and here are some I have found in the field. How would you like to swap your price problem for any of these?

Stock shortages – chronic inability to supply. Sudden and unexplained changes in management – your boss just disappears. The sales staff has lost confidence in the main product line. The service department, already overworked, is cut by half. A salesman, chosen by his colleagues to point out genuine grievan- ces to management, is fired. Promotion is *always* done from outside the company – whenever there is a plum job to be filled, some clown is brought in.

Another look at price

How do you like those pumpkins? Is the only problem that you have a higher price than the enemy? (Please don't tell me that this is not a problem, it's an opportunity – that sort of artificially-positive nonsense merely irritates me). Then be happy; you are in good shape and good company, because the best salesmen seem to sell the high-priced products, and that's a fact.

COFFEE-BREAK 3: PSSST – WANNA MAKE SOME EASY MONEY? INCREASE A SALE'S UNIT VALUE

Well, it *is* easy money, really. Easy, that is, compared with going out and grabbing a sale cold turkey. What we are concerned with here is the situation where the customer (and he is already a customer, notice, not merely a prospect) has already bought or ordered something and paid or is ready to pay, say, one hundred quid. We are going to do something here which will persuade him to part with *two* hundred. We have therefore not created a new sale but have increased the value of the present sale, okay?

I suppose this is where it is easiest to distinguish between the virgin salesman and the old pro. The new boy hears the man say: 'Fine! It looks good. Put me down for a dozen.' Holy cow! It dawns on him that he has made a sale; a *sale*, do you hear me, Mabel? A SALE! He barely manages to get out of the customer's office before letting loose with a 'Yeeeeooowww!!!', and he beats it to his manager's office to lay this offering at his feet.

In the same situation the old pro nods, thanks the customer for the order (without going overboard with his gratitude – he knows that the buying decision was made not for the salesman's benefit but for the buyer's), and shifts to a new tack. The sale isn't over yet, by a long chalk. When he walks out he has additional orders in his brief-case – and these were obtained without moving an inch, without finding another prospect, without having to do any further credit investigations, and without raising a sweat.

Truly, it is easy money.

There are three ways to increase the unit value of a sale. Depending on what you sell and who you sell it to, one or more of them will apply to you. Study them and decide which is for you, and then determine that you will never walk away from a customer without trying to increase the value of the sale which you have just written.

If there is anyone out there who fears from what he has just read that we are going to increase the value of the sale by high-pressuring the poor customer, well, I'm not even going to bother to deny it. Read on and find out for yourself that what we are doing here is in fact honest and helpful selling.

Way one: Sell bigger lots

You have a customer who is a regular buyer, Lord bless him. He buys five cases of product every two weeks, and isn't it nice to have that order turning up every fortnight? That's fine, but have you thought how much better it would be if instead of five cases every two weeks he gave us an order of ten cases every four weeks!

How would this help us, since we would not be selling him any more product than we do now? It would help in several ways:

- It would mean more economical deliveries – half as many, with a full truck.

- It costs plenty to process an order through your company – ask your accountant – and less paperwork is more efficient.

- Twice as much of our product in the customer's stockroom means less space for the opposition's products – it has the effect of keeping the opposition's sales down.

This is all very well, but none of this is of any interest to our customer; this is good news for *us*, not for him. How do we persuade him to go along with the idea of larger orders?

- Half the *number* of orders means half the invoices, delivery notes and other paperwork.

- Half the *number* of deliveries means less hassle for his staff.

- More stock in his stockroom means less chance of running out of stock, and this could be an expensive nuisance for him.

Try this way of increasing the value of the sale; show him the advantages for him. What can he do? He can say 'No', and wouldn't that be a terrible thing? 'No' leaves no bruises. If you get one 'Yes' out of five tries you are still ahead of the game.

Way two: Sell across the range

Every salesman who has a *range* of products as distinct from the man who has one or two speciality lines, has some real favourites in the range. These are products which he loves selling; he gets a real kick out of talking about them, showing them and selling them. Then, and we are all guilty of this, he has a few products which as far as he is concerned his company can stuff down a rathole. He doesn't like them, he hates even talking about them and in fact he pretends they don't exist. As you can imagine, he doesn't sell many of them.

I am talking straight at myself on this subject. I can well remember times when I simply pushed certain of my product lines under the rug. In one case when I was selling life insurance I decided that short-term endowment was a particularly stupid type of insurance and as far as I was concerned it didn't appear in my rate-book.

When we do this, when we fail to sell across the range of our products, we are deliberately restricting our potential sales figures. We sell four when we could *just as easily* sell five; we take an order for a thousand pounds when an additional five hundred pounds is within our reach.

Why? Why do we turn our backs on these products and therefore these additional sales? Well, why did I not like short-term endowment policies? It was because I saw them as providing very expensive cover and comparatively low interest on the money. It was not until my new business manager pointed out that while that was true as far as it went there were some applications for which this type of insurance was perfect. The same day that all this dawned on me I sold my first short-term endowment policy – but the point is that I sold it to a man who had just bought a straight life policy from me, so this was an additional sale which I would not have got. And please remember, I got it without having to find another prospect, without using a teaspoon more petrol or one more step of shoe-leather or stirring from the chair. Truly, easy money.

If you have any orphan products in your range – and if you have you will be able to identify them by the fact that the prochures for them are the ones crumpled up in the boot of your car – then do yourself a favour and pull them out. Have a long and careful look at them. Ask those colleagues of yours who seem to sell them well, just how they go about it. Ask your manager or the technical people in your company. Find out *all* about them and then go out and sell the hell out of them.

Way three: Sell related products

Today a man will buy a car. Only next month will he realise that he should have had a radio and a sunroof fitted.

Today a plant engineer will buy six control valves. Tomorrow he will telephone a different supplier for the couplings without which they are useless to him.

Today a pharmacist will order three cases of vitamin pills. He will never know that had he ordered five cases he would have got a five per cent discount and a free display stand.

What have these three examples in common? Sloppy selling, I'm afraid. These salesmen were very happy to take the orders, but they neglected to ask themselves one little question, and as a result they lost the chance of increasing the value of each sale. Here's the question; ask yourself this question every time you take an order and I promise you, you will increase your sales figures with no extra effort at all:

'WHAT GOES WITH THIS PRODUCT?'

Think about the products you sell. What goes with them? What related items make them safer, easier to use, more comfortable, better looking, more durable, more effective, better tasting?

Here, also, we have the answer to any worries that this coffee-break was a thinly-disguised way of high-pressuring or over-selling the customer. Take that plant engineer and his control

[131]

valves, for instance; when he had to get the couplings from another source, who do you think he was cursing? Did your ears burn if you had sold him the valves?

I was informed rather severely by a delegate to one of my sales clinics that: 'When someone has had the goodness to buy something from me, I don't trespass on his goodwill by trying to load him with other products.' Wow! That's an interesting way of looking at the selling business. In the first place, no single customer ever bought from me because of goodness; as Mae West said, goodness had nothing to do with it. He bought because he decided that I had the product which suited him under the circumstances which applied at that time. In the second place if a salesman believes that selling something is trespassing on the customer's goodwill then the sooner he pulls out of selling the better for everybody.

Haven't you ever heard your wife say, after a visit to the beauty counter to buy make-up base: 'Oh, I'm out of eye-liner. Now, why didn't the assistant remind me?' Who does she blame? The salesperson, of course; who else?

Look at it another way. When you go to your dentist with an aching tooth, what does he do before he picks up the drill to fix it? Right – he looks at every tooth in your mouth. Now, you don't say to him: 'Get away from me, you high-pressure artist! Stop trying to make the job more expensive; just do the tooth I came in for.' He asks himself: 'What goes with it?' – And so should we.

Pssst – wanna make some easy money? Then sell bigger lots, sell across the range, sell related products.

It's a doddle.

14

'Prove it!'

Would you believe it, we have got most of the way through the selling process. We have done this without going through reams of techniques; we have simply looked into people's heads and tried to find out why they do things. Now we will look at an aspect of selling which I truly believe separates the best from the rest. You can leave a lot out of your sales presentation but you dare not leave this out or you will not make a sale.

First you may recall that some time back I promised to give you the guts of the entire selling process in one sentence. Now is the time to do it and here it is:

PEOPLE WILL BUY WHAT YOU SELL IF YOU CAN SHOW THEM THAT THE PRODUCT WILL GIVE THEM WHAT THEY WANT – BUT BEFORE THEY BUY YOU WILL HAVE TO PRODUCE PROOF THAT WHAT YOU CLAIM IS TRUE.

That's it, that's all there is, there isn't any more. That is the guts of the selling process, and everything else is decoration. Selling is SIMPLE; this is the only string on my harp and I keep plucking away at it. Selling is a simple process. Not easy, never easy, but simple.

Very well, we have spent some time on the first half of that sentence, now we have to look at the second half – we have to prove that what we say is true. We can do this in any one of three ways:

- Let someone else prove it.
- Let something else prove it.
- let the customer prove it for himself.

Those are the three ways, and if you can become skilful at using them – and there's no reason in the world why you shouldn't because, Lord knows, they are simple enough – you can sell against the toughest opposition. You can sell where there was no apparent sale to be had, you can sell where it seemed that your product had nothing which the competitive product didn't have. Sound too good to be true? Believe it, it's true. Come with me and see.

The 'Horace Had Dandruff, Too' Method

One of the most effective ways of proving anything is to get some-one else to prove it for you, to bring in the experience of someone right outside your company to back up your claims. Perhaps you have already used this type of 'referral' selling and if so you know just how strong it can be. If not, take a moment to think how many things you have bought for the one reason that you heard about them from friends or family or business associates.

It is often said that the most effective advertising is the kind you don't pay for, and this is exactly what we are talking about. The detergent companies can spend millions for TV advertising to extol the virtues of their washing powder, and does it have any effect? Maybe, maybe not; but let Mrs Nexdore tell how it got the bloodstains out of her teacloths when nothing else could do the job and there is instant acceptance and belief.

Which is fine, but we can't leave it to the neighbours or friends of our prospects to tell them how good our products are. We have to do it ourselves; so let's do it ourselves. Starting right now, build up a dossier of stories about how your product helped people, companies, hospitals, councils and organisations to do things a little better than they were able to do before. I mean a real dossier, not something in your head; use a notebook or a file or an index – something where you can actually and physically put instances where others have benefited from using, buying, prescribing, recommending or having products sold by you.

I used a three-ring binder when I was selling pension funds, and I had those see-through clear plastic envelopes in it with letters from clients who had bought the funds from me. I promise you that those letters brought me in business which otherwise I would not have got within a mile of; in most cases all that I had to do was produce them at the right time and the game was won.

I admit to being a bit of a nut about this type of 'testimonial' letter because I have seen it work, time and time again, in cases where nothing else had the slightest effect on the listener. It is a tremendously powerful motivator to buy when you can show that others in the same situation and with the same problems as the listener overcame them by doing exactly what you are recommending. Examples:

- 'Acme Transport was going through rear axles like a chicken eating corn until they changed to this special heavy-duty transmission oil. As you see from the site superintendent's letter they had the same problem as you – climbing out of a quarry with a full load of granite.'

- 'Do you see in the second paragraph that the company secretary of Apex Mills found that once they had introduced the air-conditioning their staff turnover dropped from sixteen per cent to less than five?'

- 'I was delighted when I saw that the office manager of Amor Cosmetics mentioned our service in his letter. He was impressed with the speed and courtesy of the technicians who maintain his office copiers.'

Find someone who had the same situation as the prospect and let him read the actual words written by that person. When he sees that hell, Horace had dandruff, too, before he used this product, he is convinced in a way that you, the salesman, never could convince him.

Whenever I introduce the subject of 'testimonial' letters to a group of salesmen there is an uncomfortable feeling in the group; not always, and not with everyone, but sometimes and with some of them. The thought is, sure, we can see how the letters would work, but we don't like the idea of asking our present customers for them. Isn't that just a bit pushy? It sounds a bit as though we are saying: 'I am going to spread your name all over this town in order to flog my wares.'

[135]

A very natural reaction, and I must admit that the first few times I asked for a letter I did it with a clear line to the door, ready to disappear immediately the customer showed any sign of wanting to clobber me. I won't try to fool you; I did indeed get some refusals, but I promise you that not once did I get anything like an offended reaction. Some people said quite openly that they felt that their company would not like to have its letterhead used in that way; some said that they would be a little embarrassed if anyone phoned them to check up on the letter. But I never got anyone showing anger or annoyance.

The fact is, and I didn't expect this but it happened, most of the customers were actually flattered that I had seen fit to ask them. I remember one customer literally blushing! Kid you not. He said: 'Do you mean that you think people will be influenced to buy because of my letter?' It really is most interesting to see the reactions; often I have had the customer take as much care over the draft of the letter as he would for an application for a job.

One thing you will certainly get and you may as well be ready for it: a customer will say to you, 'Sure, why not? But *you* write the letter, and I'll get my secretary to type it and I'll sign it.' Now, that sounds marvellous, but my feeling is that if possible we should resist the temptation to spread ourselves in a flowery letter of fulsome praise for our product. The problem is, or it could be, that if the prospect phones the customer he may just ask: 'Did you actually write that letter?' – and the danger always exists that the customer will laugh and say: 'Hell, no; Beer wrote it and I signed it.' Scratch one potential sale, serve up one helping of humble pie.

The 'Horace Had Dandruff, Too' method is powerful, effective and easy to use; use it.

The 'Selling The System' Method

Has it occurred to you that you never merely sell a product? Nobody ever buys just a product, nobody ever sells one. Behind that product, whatever it may be, stands an entire *system*, and whenever we buy a product we buy the system too. This system consists of the whole complex maze of product design, manufacture, packaging, service, technical back-up, quality control, distribution, sales outlets, dealer network, advertising, promotion, merchandising, and so on and so on and so on.

It is when a salesman realises that behind every product he sells is this system that he understands what a powerful weapon he has in producing *proof*. To almost every question about the claims the salesman makes, almost every time the customer says or implies: 'Oh, yeah? Who says that what you say is true?' he can be answered with something from the *system*. Examples? Any amount of them, all implicitly questioning your claims:

Q. 'I work all over the country; how do I know that I'll always be able to get service?'
A. 'Go anywhere you like, you will never be further than two hundred miles from a service depot of ours.'
Q. 'I've been had like that before; you talk me into standardising on your line and then bingo, you change the model on me.'
A. 'We give you a written guarantee that we will hold the line for at least ten years after your last purchase.'
Q. 'I'll never sell ten cases of this stuff! There just isn't that much demand in this area.'
A. 'There will be, when you have taken advantage of our co-operative advertising campaign. It gives you customised advertising at half the cost to you.'
Q. 'No way. I don't say my staff are stupid, but they won't be able to figure out how to use this new cash register. It won't speed up flow through the check-out counters, it'll produce a bottleneck which will chase my customers away.'
A. 'Not when your people have been through our free training school. We fetch them and bring them back, and we'll even provide temporary staff to take over from them while they are learning.'
Q. 'You can't promise me that I will be getting over eleven per cent from this unit trust in five year's time.'
A. 'That is absolutely correct; nobody can predict that far ahead. but here is a graph showing the interest rates paid on this particular investment over the past twenty years, and as you see it has never fallen below eleven per cent.'

As you see, all those examples are solid, reliable proof – and they all come from some part of the *system*.

It makes sense for every salesman to sit down with plenty of paper and plenty of time and ask himself: What do I sell, each time I sell a product? What is there in the system that makes my product claims convincing, irrefutable and *believable*? If you try this exercise you will be astounded at the many goodies that go with your product, and don't forget that he *buys* the product, but the goodies come free!

Never merely sell the product; *always* sell the whole system.

The 'See For Yourself' Method

I love this one. I love it not only because it works so well but also it is the final confirmation that selling truly is a simple process. You want him to believe? You want to produce proof? So *show* him! You can hardly get anything more simple than that. Sometimes the magic in a sales presentation starts right here. Sometimes the sales talk starts *working* when the salesman stops *talking*. Stop talking, and start showing, and so often, everything begins to come together. He finally believes when he sees; the proof is there in front of his eyes. End of story.

I don't intend to go on and on about this way of getting proof across to the prospect; I am not going to insult your intelligence. Of *course* he believes the evidence of his own eyes! How can he not? All I should like to emphasise is the fairly obvious point that when you are showing your product, what it looks like, how it works, how simple and robust and smooth and yellow and light and flexible and beautiful it is, *pulleeease* make sure that you know what you're doing. He is watching you like a ferret, and he would love to see you make a twit of yourself. Why not? Anything for a laugh. So you will have rehearsed your one-man show before the curtain rises, won't you?

You didn't like that last metaphor? Does it sound too much as though you are putting on an act when you use this method? But of course you are putting on an act! Why not, when there is nothing hypocritical about it? You genuinely believe in your product, don't you? Well, what you are doing is getting him to believe in it, too, and if the best way is to act it out for him instead of talking it out, well, go for it!

[138]

Oh, yes, you are acting here. At this stage of the presentation the overture comes to its end, the drums roll, the spotlights shine, the audience leans forward in its seats, the curtain rises – and there you stand, turning the handle of your franking machine while the envelopes fly out in all directions to the frenzied applause of your fans.

All right, I went overboard there, but I'm not crossing it out because I don't care what it takes to convince you that this part of the presentation can produce excitement in the prospect as no other can.

How you go about the 'See For Yourself' method depends on your personality and your imagination, but it may be worthwhile to mention only one refinement. When I was selling a range of high-priced consumer products, we had a saying: 'Get him to *hold* it and you've almost *sold* it.' You see, don't you, that if you can get the prospect to participate in some way it produces a reality in his mind which is much stronger than if he is merely a spectator.

However you do it, whatever personal subtleties you bring in to this method, I promise you that the 'showers' in any sales team will always beat the 'blowers'. Show him! Show him with confidence and love and a fire in your belly, and he will gain the excitement from you, he will believe – and he will buy.

15

Which is better?
Selling by comparison

Try this sometime: go into a salesroom of some sort; perhaps a motorcar showroom. Walk up to one of the gleaming cars on the floor and examine it. Sooner or later (in most cases, I'm afraid, later rather than sooner), a salesman will wander up and stand at your elbow. When you have his attention, ask him something like this: 'Tell me, how does this car compare with the Warthog GT?' Pick a car which you happen to know is the salesman's toughest competition.

The reaction you will get will vary from one extreme to the other. On the one side the salesman will say: 'Oh, I'm sorry; I couldn't possibly comment of the Warthog. I sell the Roebuck, as you can see, and it just wouldn't be ethical of me to discuss the opposition. I'm sure you understand, sir.' What a *nice* young man, and what fine moral fibre! We shall come back to him.

Then on the other end of the scale of course we will get the character who will say: 'The Warthog GT? Get serious – don't you know that they are recalling all Warthogs because the back axles are catching fire and burning all the passengers to a crisp?'

The second example there is your basic 'knocker'; a fairly common species and of no particular interest to us except to identify and avoid. No, it is the first example which we must examine, because his philosophy is much more profound, and much more dangerous, than that of our happy knocker.

On the face of it the man who says: 'I won't discuss my opposition. I refuse to run down their products; I sell honestly, by talking about the advantages of my own products and letting the customer make up his own mind,' is a good salesman. Good in

[140]

two ways, too; first, he is an ethical person, and second, he is probably competent at his job, since he concentrates on the good news about his own products instead of talking about the bad news of the opposition's – very positive selling, and three cheers for him.

It doesn't work that way. I know it sounds good, but that is simply not professional selling, and you can prove it for yourself. Staying on the motorcar example, let us suppose that you are in the process of buying a new car. You have examined the various makes and have reduced your short list to two, the Warthog and the Roebuck. You go to the showroom of the Roebuck to take a closer look at the car. Now, one of the things you wish to discover is the comparative fuel economy of the two vehicles; you therefore ask the salesman the simple question: 'How does your fuel consumption compare with that of the Warthog?'

It's a reasonable question, isn't it? Of course it is. You are not asking the salesman to run down the Warthog by telling you that it has a thirst like an Australian bushranger. Nor do you want him to tell you that the Roebuck will run a hundred miles on a pint of dirty dishwater; you want an honest answer. Think about it – before you buy, you have a right to know the answer to this sort of question, haven't you? Yes, you have! And the salesman who tries to put you off by saying self-righteously that he doesn't dirty himself by talking about the guys across the street is not giving you the information you want and deserve.

What should he have done, our Roebuck salesman? Well, how would you have felt if he had said something like this: 'That's an important point; we all worry about the price of petrol these days. Here is a book of road-tests of this year's models. Let's see what an independent source says about the two cars.' You know how you would have felt – you would have realised that a professional salesman was not trying to con you but was giving you information you wanted and that you had to have before making a buying decision.

I dare not go on until I have answered a question which I am sure is in your mind at this moment: 'All right, so he shows me the comparative fuel consumption figures, and he falls down dead when his opposition is better than his car. What happens then?' Nothing very dramatic happens, and he certainly doesn't fall down dead. The pro simply says: 'As you can see, the Warthog is better by about two per cent. While we have the two tests in front of us, let's look at the passenger space; if you have a family you will appreciate this. Also, as you see, the cost of service is particularly low with the Roebuck, and I'm sure that this would be important to you . . .' Not only is our salesman not dismayed by the small advantage of the opposition on one point but he uses the opportunity to go into a very competent sales presentation.

There will always be certain aspects of any product where the enemy has the inside track on you. Fine; all you do is acknowledge this and move on to another aspect.

To get back to the concept of discussing opposition products: whether you like it or not it has to be done. Look at it this way: when someone is about to buy something – and we're not talking about a box of matches but something important – how does he buy? Well, he looks at one product then another and perhaps another. He goes back to the first product, then he remembers something about the third product, then he makes a note about something in the second product, then he phones the salesman to ask about something to do with the first product. What is he *doing*? It deserves a line to itself:

HE IS BUYING BY COMPARISON

That's right, he is buying by comparing the merits of one product with another. We all do this, don't we? It is the only sensible way to buy. Now, if he is *buying* by comparison then our job is clear, and give this a line by itself, too:

WE HAVE TO SELL BY COMPARISON

We have no choice; we really and truly have no choice. It is a basic axiom of communication that if you wish to get through to someone you have to speak his language – you must be on the same plane, you need to stay on his level. If he is buying by comparing and we are trying to sell without comparing we are doomed to failure.

To put it another way, he is buying in a two-dimensional situation, ours and our opposition's, and we are selling in a one-dimensional situation, ours only. How can we possibly succeed? We can't succeed.

Which is better? Selling by comparison

All right, if you are still with me on this point then the only thing to decide on is exactly *how* we are to sell by comparison. We are not going to knock the opposition, neither directly nor by innuendo. We are not going to drag the opposition into the sales talk unless it is already in – that is, unless the prospect has come right out and mentioned it by name or has indicated in some way that he is interested in it.

Before we can compare one product with another we have to see exactly what we have in our product which will make sense to the prospect, and compare this with what the other product has. Let us be crystal clear on one point; it is no use grabbing a piece of paper and shoving down a list of all the good points about our product and then on the other side of the paper, putting down all the weak points of the opposition. That may look very nice and cosy but it won't impress the prospect. What we are engaged in here is *product analysis*, and it has to be completely honest and balanced or it won't have the slightest effect. No, I'm wrong there; it will have an effect. It will cause the prospect to give us a belly-laugh and throw us out.

I call this method of analysing two competitive products the 'GO – STOP' system, and while it is simplicity itself to do it requires a little explanation as to how it works. There is of course nothing new in the idea of comparing one product with another; pretty well every sales course does it. What makes mine different is that in it we recognise that what excites Charlie can leave Horace cold – or even turn him off. Remember when we started I said that we would work the other way around from most sales training courses? Even here, where we are working so very close to the *products*, we still say: 'Why should he want it?' Rather than: 'It's got this, so it will do this – and the heck with whether he wants it or not.' We might as well take the example of two motorcars rather than two turret lathes or two semi-conductors since we all drive cars and we can therefore relate to the points used in the comparison.

As you see, the 'GO – STOP' system is almost self-explanatory. The top half, the GO part, consists of those points which we feel would attract the prospect to the product, while the bottom half, the STOP part, includes those which will repel him. Both parts are divided in half, the left half being for our product and the right for the opposition. So far, a fairly conventional product analysis

[143]

sheet. But now we introduce a new dimension. You see the numbers from five to one down the middle of the sheet? This is a rating scale, and here we ask ourselves: 'Who and what is our prospect? What does he want from the product? *And how important is that to him?*'

Back we go inside the head of our prospect. It is not enough that we are able to analyse the product and say: 'Hey – look at all the great things it's got! Let's rush out and sell the living daylights out of them.' Oh, no; we are much more sophisticated than that. We realise that even when two people can be impressed or excited by the same thing, *it can have different degrees of importance to them*. Another thing; the same thing about a product can be important to different people *for different reasons*!

I once bought a small 'fun' car; not much more than a toy, really. I loved it because it was great fun to drive; you could throw it about like a motor-cycle. My wife liked it because it was the easiest thing in the world to park – it would fit in anywhere. My gardener was pleased because he could wash it practically standing on one spot, it was so small. Three people, one product; one aspect of that product (its size), three reasons for liking the product.

So, the 'GO – STOP' analysis sheet has been filled in as you see, but it doesn't help us much until we know who we are selling to. Let us say that our prospect is Hyram Fribble, a fifty-four year old insurance broker with a low back problem, a large wife and a gung-ho son at University. Probably (and we only say 'probably' until we know him better) the product analysis would suit his wants and needs pretty well as it is.

Because we have done this analysis honestly, we have not tried to disguise the fact that the Warthog has some very good things going for it; if we don't acknowledge this and put these things down on the analysis sheet we are simply playing games. We have also recognised that there are things about our product which Mr Fribble will not like. If we expect to sell to him we have to write down and examine them to see what we can do about them.

Do I need to make the point that the 'GO – STOP' sheet is *not* a sales talk? We do not show the sheet to the prospect; it is none of his business. This is a working piece of paper from which we shall be extracting a sales presentation, based on our knowledge of our product, of our opposition's product, and of our prospective customer.

OUR PRODUCT		THEIR PRODUCT
ROEBUCK		WARTHOG

'GO' Factors

OUR PRODUCT		THEIR PRODUCT
Conservative design	5	Sample, robust engine
Orthopaedically-designed seats	4	Power steering
Excellent service facilities	3	High resale value
Large luggage space	2	Central locking device
Good fuel economy	1	Comprehensive instrumentation

'STOP' Factors

OUR PRODUCT		THEIR PRODUCT
High service costs	5	New, untried dealer network
Highly advanced complex engine	4	Unduly hard seats
No anti-lock braking system	3	Sporting racy design
Acceleration not very impressive	2	New model coming out next year
Seats not fully-reclining	1	Not available with metallic paint

To me the main advantage of this method is not that it gives us anything new; we had all the information here before we started to fill the sheet in. What it does, and it does it graphically and dramatically, is to present a *picture* of precisely what it is that we have that we can sell, compared to what the opposition can sell. It does more than that, too. When I created the 'GO – STOP' method for my own use it dawned on me that perhaps the most useful part of it was that it actually gave me a very good idea of what the opposition sales talk would be! Think about it – if you know the strongest sales points of the enemy, and you have also acknowledged that your own product has some points which are not as strong as some of his, *then you know what he is going to say*. He will be using his strong sales points, certainly, but he will also be bearing down on your weak points.

This is the real edge this system gives you – you will be hit with no unpleasant surprises in any competitive selling situation.

Now, let us go back to Hyram Fribble and his family. What do we know about him? Not a great deal at the moment, but we shall be learning more as we talk to him and ask him questions. In the meantime we have to do some assuming.

He is a middle-aged insurance broker, so unless he is a closet Walter Mitty, a solid and conservative design to the car could appeal to him as projecting the right image. He has low back pain and the orthopaedically-correct seats will be a real hot point in the talk. Service facilities must be important; he is unlikely to want to stick his head under the bonnet and scratch around there himself, and even less would this be so for his wife.

As we go down the Power Scale the points become less important; we can assume that while reasonable luggage space is a good thing to have it would not weigh heavily in his mind. Insurance brokers are seldom to be found standing in a queue outside a soup-kitchen, so we can take it that fuel economy ranks somewhat low in his scale of values.

Looking at the STOP factors of our product we see that there are things which will not impress him very much. We must be ready to counter them if he raises them. We can meet the problem of high service costs by using our twelve words (do you remember them? Go back to our chat about price), and the fact that our power unit is state-of-the-art and mechanically complex can be countered by talking about our highly-trained and skilful technical staff.

As for the STOP factors on the 2 and 1 sections of the Power Scale, we don't see them as being very important. He isn't likely to want to enter the car in a drag race, and although the comfort of the seats is a major factor with him, the chances of his wanting to recline them fully and go to sleep in them are remote.

All well and good, and we are ready to sell Mr Fribble. We shall be watching him as we talk and listening very carefully as he talks, so that we can shift the emphasis of our sales points if this should become necessary. If for instance we find him sitting behind the wheel with a gleam in his eye and the posture of an Emerson Fittipaldi then we shall certainly direct our talk to roadholding and cornering. (We can't swank about the vivid acceleration of our car because there isn't any.)

But suppose we were selling to Hyram Fribble Junior, the macho third-year science student? Suppose his father had sent him along to our showroom to have a look and give his opinion? Then we have a very different situation. Firstly, our Power Scale goes completely haywire, since we can't see him getting excited about our conservative design. If he will be borrowing his dad's car then, depending whether or not he is expected to pay for his own petrol, fuel economy could be a factor. Do you see that depending on whom we are talking to, we could have a STOP factor turning into a GO factor and vice versa? The hard seats and sporting design of the opposition car could easily be GO factors for young Fribble. (We know nothing about his social activities, but the lack of fully-reclining seats could put a real damper on his after-hours projects.)

Similarly, for Mrs Fribble with her well-endowed and generously-proportioned frame, we would beam our talk heavily in the direction of comfort and ease of driving.

And that is the 'GO – STOP' method of product analysis. There is nothing magical about it, but it has worked for me and for thousands of my trainees. It forces the salesman to look at the product through the eyes of the *customer*, rather than those of the product designer, the advertising agency, the marketing executives or the salesman himself.

If it does nothing else it has the tremendous advantage that it prepares you for the sales interview, and as Louis Pasteur said: 'Opportunity favours the mind that is prepared to receive it.'

Count on it.

COFFEE-BREAK 4: YOU GOTTA BELIEVE!
THE POWER OF PRODUCT CONFIDENCE

This was told to me by the sales manager of a team of Yellow Pages salespeople. As you probably know, a Yellow Pages salesman calls on present customers – those firms who have already advertised – as well as prospective customers. The idea of seeing existing advertisers is to persuade them to advertise again in the forthcoming edition, and, if possible, to upgrade their present advertisements.

He sent one of his virgins out into the territory to call on the companies which specialised in heavy industrial equipment, and this new boy was not having fun. Wherever he went he got the same reaction: 'No way; you can't sell heavy equipment, capital goods, high unit cost products, through the Yellow Pages. That sort of advertising is fine for plumbers and lawnmower repair shops but not for us. Go away and quit bothering us.'

He was brand new to the selling business and, as you can imagine, this sort of reaction was slowly destroying his morale and breaking his heart. By the end of the week he had not had a single new sale nor had he managed to upgrade any of the old advertisers. The few customers he had managed to keep had agreed grudgingly and without enthusiasm. On the Friday he was about ready to hang himself. He walked into the office of a man who sold enormous dry-cleaning machines. This company had had a sixteenth-page advertisement in the previous edition, and while the salesman had no hope of upgrading (you can't sell capital equipment through the Yellow Pages), he hoped forlornly to hold on to the sixteenth-page.

He introduced himself, identified the purpose of his visit and was filled with terror when the prospect jumped up and reached

[148]

out for him with the apparent intention of grabbing his throat and strangling him. Instead, he grabbed the salesman by the shoulder. 'You!' he said, hoarse with emotion. 'You are with the Yellow Pages?' The salesman admitted it, with his past life flashing before his eyes. 'I have an advertisement in the Yellow Pages!' the man exclaimed. The salesman confirmed the fact, feeling that the only decent thing to do would be for him to refund the cost of the advertisement out of his own pocket. The prospect took a firmer grip on the salesman's shoulder. 'Do you know?' he said, shaking a finger in the salesman's face, 'Do you have any idea how many machines I have sold because of that silly little advertisement? Can you imagine how many leads my salespeople have had from that one insertion?'

Our salesman began to realise that he was in no fear of death – the speaker was cutting off the flow of blood to his shoulder not in anger but in joy. He recovered his composure, or as much of it as was available to him after the trauma of the introduction, and when he walked out of the office he had a signed order for a half-page – eight times the size of the previous advertisement.

Well, nine feet tall and with the flourish of victory trumpets still ringing in his ears, he walked into the next prospect. He introduced himself. 'Forget it, buddy,' said the man. 'You can't sell heavy equipment through the Yellow Pages.'

Our salesman smiled broadly. 'Oh, yes you can,' he said. 'Let me tell you about it!'

What had changed that salesman from a timorous, cowering beastie to a conquistador? Product confidence, that's all. He now *knew* that his product worked, and he was not about to take any negative opinions from anybody. He *believed*, and if you are to be a creative salesman you gotta believe.

I once went back to a service station to collect my car after its regular service, and while I was there I saw another model being serviced. I had heard of this model but had never seen it, so I strolled over and asked the mechanic: 'Tell me – what's this car like? I've heard so much about it.' The mechanic looked over his shoulder and approached his mouth to my ear. 'Rubbish!' he whispered.

Well, he was bulging with muscles and I am a man of peace or a coward, whichever, so I didn't carry on the conversation, such as it was (I have cleaned up his remark – it was three letters shorter and three times ruder). But what I felt like saying was: 'My friend, go and put on your jacket and pick up your cards and leave this company. Don't delay, do it today, and go and find a place where you can work on something which you don't think is rubbish. Go on; do it. You will be doing this company a favour because feeling the way you do you can't be doing very good work, and you will be doing a favour for yourself, because you don't really have much of a future here.' Imagine that poor guy – every morning of his life he has to get out of bed and go and work on something which he believes is rubbish.

You realise that whether or not the car was a good product has nothing to do with it; the point is that *he* had no faith in the product.

I say to you, and every good sales manager would agree with me: ask yourself whether you really believe in the products which you sell. A good criterion is: Would I sell them with confidence to a close friend? If you decide that you lack any real confidence in your product range, don't give up yet; go deeply into the reasons for your lack of confidence; you could just find that it stems from lack of depth product knowledge. If so, the solution is simple. But if after all you find that you really don't believe in what you sell then do yourself and the company a favour, and leave. Out there is a product you can believe in and sell with confidence and a fire in the belly. Find it, and find the joy in selling which every salesman deserves.

You gotta believe!

16

The sales talk
– customer-dominated
or salesman-controlled?

Why is so much of the money, time and effort spent on sales training simply wasted? I am a sales trainer, don't forget, and I tell you that more than half of all sales training has not the slightest beneficial effect. More correctly, over half of the salesmen who go through some form of sales training don't get any real benefit from it.

Why not? The techniques which are taught have been sanctified by time and use, and although I don't believe in them myself there must be some good in them or people wouldn't keep teaching them. Yet when the salesman goes out and tries to use those same techniques which he agreed to in the conference room he so often falls on his face. Why?

Well, there may be many reasons, but I believe that the main reason is a simple one:

THE CUSTOMER DOMINATES THE SALES TALK

And when he does, the poor salesman has as much chance of selling as I have of landing the lead part in *Annie Get Your Gun*.

Yes, the customer takes over the sales talk. He dominates it, he decides which way it will go, he makes his points and will not allow the salesman to make his, and he cuts it off just when he decides that he has had enough. Those sexy techniques which the salesman has learnt (most of them off by heart, Lord help him) avail him nought, for the simple reason that he never gets around to using them.

We must not allow the customer to dominate the talk. When you think about it, the talk isn't his, anyway; it's ours. We say this not in an arrogant way but because it is the truth. The sales talk belongs to the salesman, not the customer, and he should be running it. Of course, we don't want a salesman-dominated talk, either; there should be no domination on either side. What, therefore, do we want? We want a salesman-*controlled* talk; that's more like it!

Before we talk about how to achieve the salesman-controlled talk I am going to put down as much of a sales talk as I can stand. This talk is not made up, it actually happened, and I had to stand and listen to it happening. The memory is still painful. When I can't take any more I shall cut it off. My comments are in italics, although of course I didn't open my mouth during the actual interview. The strain it puts on trainers who have to stand mute and listen to mangled sales talks is responsible for the high suicide rate amongst us.

'Good morning, Mr Hill; I'm Charlie Week, of Pinnacle Supplies. I called on you last month but you were rather busy at the time. You probably don't remember.' (*A hell of a way to start a sales talk! It simply invites the reaction which follows.*)

'No I don't, and I'm still busy. What can I do for you?'

'Well, it's rather a case of what I can do for you, Mr Hill.' (*This is the sort of smart-arse remark which doesn't move the sales talk any further forward and only irritates the listener – this listener is already irritated enough.*) 'My company has produced a new control unit which I think you will be interested in.'

'Not another control unit! Every time I try to standardise, you guys bring out a new model!' (*Now, that is interesting; this man has problems with standardisation. If the salesman is on the ball he will pick this up. I hope against hope.*)

'Well, we have to try to keep up to date, and this new unit has some features which I think you will like.'

'*And* a higher price, too, I expect.' (*This is a clear attempt by the prospect to dominate the talk. He is putting on record his resistance to price even before it is mentioned by the salesman.*

[152]

Customer-dominated or salesman-controlled?

The salesman's answer to this will largely decide how the talk will proceed from here on. I am holding my breath – you do, too.)

'Well, I admit the price is a little higher, of course –' (*Sweet Saint Agnes, Charlie – couldn't you think of a better word than 'admit'? You have immediately lain on your back with your paws in the air in the classic attitude of surrender. He is now well in the driving seat. If you can recover from your defensive position you will have accomplished a near-miracle.*)

'All right, let's look at it now that you're here, but I don't really need any control units right now.' (*Well, that's something. He is prepared to look and listen, and that, if you think about it, means that he is not completely happy with the products he is using now. Also, he could be in the market for more. 'I don't really* need' *is not the same as 'I don't need.'*)

'No, I expect you don't, but if you should need some in the future –' (*Charlie, Charlie, Charlie; do you realise what you have done? You have absolutely guaranteed that whatever else may happen during this interview, you will not make a sale.*)

'All right, all right; let's get on with it. Is this it? Hell, man, it's even more complicated than the one I use now, and my men have trouble with that one!' (*At last – this is Charlie's wedge into the sale, if only he grabs at it. Do you see what the position is? This man has a real problem – his staff is having trouble with the opposition unit, and he desperately wants to avoid this. Industrial salesmen are problem-solvers, remember? Go, Charlie; go!*)

'Oh, no, Mr Hill; it's not at all more complicated!'

'Listen, Mr whatever your name is, are you trying to tell me that I don't know when a control unit is difficult to use? Let me tell you, sonny –'

Sorry, but I can't stand any more. Let us leave Charlie here; in a flash of intuitive genius he seems to have decided that arguing with the prospect is the best way of making a sale. As I said, this

[153]

talk actually happened, and it ended with the engineer simply walking away and leaving us standing there with our mouths full of teeth and the nearest sale ten thousand miles away.

This salesman had been through the sales courses, he had read the books and seen the films on selling; he was full of the techniques. Yet he got nowhere near the chance of a sale. Why? Because the prospect took the sales talk over and dominated the interview, to the extent that when we got back into the car after leaving the factory with our tails between our legs, the salesman turned to me and said wonderingly: 'Hell, do you think the unit *could* be more complicated?' Incredible! the prospect actually sold the salesman, instead of the other way around. And how did he do it? He took the sales talk over and dominated it.

We cannot allow the customer to do this. The moment he does we are lost. This is the real reason that so much sales training turns out to be a waste of time and money and effort. What is the good of learning a lot of techniques if you are never going to be allowed to use them?

As you know, I don't think much of the lists of techniques which are given to salesmen in sales courses anyhow, but at least they are better than nothing. If you have them you may as well use them; but they won't work if a listener has taken over the reins and is now in the driving seat.

How do we avoid this common and dangerous situation? Remember that we don't want to dominate the sales talk, we merely don't want the listener to dominate it. We do want to control it, because unless we do we will never get our message across. When we say 'control' the talk, this doesn't mean we don't let the prospect talk. The creative salesman knows one thing with crystal clarity, and that is that one word from the prospect is worth twenty from the salesman. Read that again, please – one word of his is worth twenty of ours. We *need* him to speak. We are in the most terrible trouble unless he speaks. Those of you who have already done some selling know that this is true – one of the most difficult characters to sell to is the Sphinx, the guy who simply sits there and grunts at you. No, we certainly don't want to stop him talking, but neither do we want to lose the initiative. How do we do it? We use the Skeleton Sales Talk. It is simple (if it was complicated it wouldn't be in this book) and it works.

The Skeleton Sales Talk

When someone asks you to make a speech at a wedding or similar function, what do you do? (Apart from desperately trying to get out of doing it, I mean.) Well, if you are really stupid you write out your speech and try to learn it by heart. This puts the curse of seven saints on your undertaking right from the start, since you will almost certainly lose your train of thought somewhere in the middle and have to improvise from there on. The audience will know exactly what has happened to you and lay bets with each other as to when you will dry up altogether.

So you don't learn it by heart. This is also, of course, the best argument against the so-called 'canned' sales talk – the one the salesman learns by heart. He will also, as the luckless speechmaker has done, lose his way somewhere along the road and have to fight through a trackless jungle to an uncertain destination. No sales trainers like the canned sales talk for the very good reason that it takes the bread out of our mouths to teach salesmen something to squawk like a parrot to every prospect they meet from there on. However, it is not only the fact that if every salesman learnt his talk by heart we would have to go straight and find an honest way of making a living which makes us hate the canned talk. The real weakness of this way of selling is that if you give the same talk to this man and that woman and those people, you are saying: 'You all have the very same needs and wants and hopes and desires and hang-ups and triumphs and disasters and glories and sins.'

If that is true – that everyone wants the same thing from a product – then the entire second half of this book is a rip-off and I should be arrested for obtaining money on false pretences. (Is it okay if you get money on *true* pretences?) It isn't true, of course it isn't true, and that is why you need the Skeleton Sales Talk.

No, you don't write your speech out in full and learn it off word for word, but you do put down some notes, and if you think about it, these notes are in the form of headlines like those of a newspaper. You put down DELIGHTED which reminds you to tell the lie about how you felt when you were asked to propose the toast. You put down FATHER CARMODY, to remind you that RABBI HALPERIN was *last* week's wedding, and for heaven's sake not to mix them up. You put down FLOWERS – THANK

AUNT FLO or there will be a rift in the family that will last all winter. You put down FRYING-PAN? DESERT ISLAND? to give you the option of two jokes, one of them slightly risqué, depending on how much champagne has been drunk before your speech. You put down MICKEY AND *MAVIS* because your wife has warned you that if you get the bride's name wrong one more time she is going to kill you.

Having done all that you write it neatly and legibly in large letters on a postcard and slide it into your cutaway so that you can sneak a last look at it while cousin Clara is singing 'I'll walk beside you'.

And that, to all intents and purposes, is the Skeleton Sales Talk.

The Skeleton Sales Talk was invented by me while sitting outside the place of business of a customer. It was in fact a service station and the customer was the owner/manager of the joint. I was stalling, really, because I was not looking forward to calling on this particular character. We didn't get along, he and I – I seemed to strike sparks off him, and he had the same effect on me as a fly in a cat's ear.

For want of something to pass the time until I had to go in I pulled out my notebook and scribbled down a few thoughts about my customer. About the problems we had had in the past, about what I was planning to say to him today, what his reaction would probably be, who else I should see on the call, and so on. I read through the few rough notes and, feeling for some reason a lot better than I had, I went onto the driveway and into the office. It was the best call I had ever had with the man. Afterwards, talking it over with my sales manager, I realised that this was at least partly because I had prepared for the call. My few rough notes were really an outline of how I planned to run the sales interview, and they helped me more than I would have thought possible.

I shall never forget a remark by a man whom I consider to be one of the finest battle commanders of World War II – Field Marshal Erwin Rommel, the famous Desert Fox of the Afrika Korps. He said: 'Time spent in reconnaissance is seldom wasted.' Golden words, when you think about them, and just as applicable to the job of a salesman as to that of a soldier.

Okay, here is a Skeleton Sales Talk, together with my comments. Please notice that I said *a* Skeleton Sales Talk, not *the* Skeleton Sales Talk. This is the sort of thing which works for me, but don't take it and try to make it your own just as it is. You and I don't sell in the same way, and your priorities are not my priorities. Also, different industries may require different headings and a different order of doing things. Look my SST over and build a better one for yourself.

What do I know about them?
Who am I seeing? What sort of character is he? What happened on the previous call? What is his involvement with my product? (Is he buying for others to use or is he directly concerned?) What are company policies and procedures which could affect the sale? WHAT DOES HE WANT THAT MY PRODUCT CAN GIVE HIM?

What is he doing now?
What opposition products is he using or has he used? What are the strong/weak points about those products? What good/bad experiences has he had from those products? What experience has he had with my company and my products? Good/bad?

What will stop him buying?
Note: this is *not* a negative-minded question! If we are to sell to him we must have an idea of what sales resistance he will put up against buying. We don't *fear* the resistance, we merely *prepare* for it.

What will prove it?
Do I tell him or show him? Are there any similar situations I can talk about? Can I use letters from other customers? Is there something about my product which I can actually bring in and put in his hands?

How shall I get action from him?
Is there some way of creating a sense of urgency to buy? Can I show him the bad news of putting things off, or will the good news of doing it now be more effective? Is there anyone else in his business who needs to pass on this decision? Can I get to him? What can I say to wrap it up finally? What will best summarise the reasons to buy in one simple sentence?

That's it. It doesn't look very dramatic or exciting, does it? Only five main questions and a lot of secondary ones. Yet I promise you that if you use the Skeleton Sales Talk the next time you have an important sales call you will enter that office or factory, shop or home with one priceless asset. You will have CONFIDENCE that your reconnaissance has not been wasted, and that opportunity will favour your prepared mind.

17

Don't feed the animals – the Customer Zoo

Let us take a break from the selling process for a while – we don't have much more to do, anyway – and sit back, loosen our collars and examine our fellow-men.

It has been an axiom of all the things we have looked at and worked with so far that people are *different*. Therefore it makes much more sense to work from the *person* to the *product* than from the product to the person, which is the way that most sales training is given. In this section we are going to be looking straight at people, and again we shall be asking the eternal questions: 'What is there about this person which I can excite? What turns him on? What turns him off? What attracts him and what repels him?' Find out the answers to these questions and you have the lever, the weapon, the chemistry to persuade.

Of all the many people that a salesman meets in his day-to-day job I have taken a round half-dozen samples so that we can do an exercise in simple analysis. I have labelled them with the names of animals to make identification easier, and I should like you to read the description of each one and then ask yourself: 'What is there about my product or my company or the system which I sell – or the salesmen who call on him – which he will love or hate?'

I have given some possible answers at the end of the Zoo, but don't cheat, now. Put your own answers down first and then see if you agree with mine.

The Squirrel

He has a high drive for SECURITY. Recognise him? The burglar-bars on his house are so thick it looks like a maximum-security prison. His riskiest sport is Scrabble. He wears his seatbelt in the car wash. He has the first pound he ever earned; he never throws anything away. He has a special file for the guarantees on all his household appliances. He knows his passport number. He carries a pocket calculator when shopping. His car was bought on a special deal and its colour doesn't show dirt.

HE WILL LIKE . Low Cost , Good Back up Security ....

HE WILL DISLIKE . High Cost , Risks, ...

The Lion

He has a high drive for STATUS. Recognise him? He is much concerned about the size of the carpet in his office. His new car is always a different one from his last one – people must realise that it's new. He would rather live in a shack with the 'right' address than a mansion with the 'wrong' one. He thinks he is an authority on wine – even if he isn't, and he always buys it by the case. He gives generously to the poor, but he would rather not see them, and certainly not around his house. His car is a majestic black – what other colour is there?

HE WILL LIKE . Sounds Good , looks , expensive ......

HE WILL DISLIKE Same - ....

The Dodo

He has a high drive for CONSERVATISM. Recognise him? He hates any form of change – for him the nineteenth century is where it's all happening. He wears sock-suspenders and separate collars. He keeps things for a long time – he won't change 'just for the sake of changing'. He talks a lot about the 'good old days' and how 'they don't make things like that any more'. He doesn't have TV – he isn't even sure about Hi-Fi. His car is a pre-war model. (What do you mean, *automatic* gearbox?)

HE WILL LIKE ... Old. Traditional

HE WILL DISLIKE ... loud, Brash,

The Peacock

He has a high drive for RECOGNITION. Recognise him? His clothes look like the Aurora Borealis. He was the first man in the office with a digital-alarm-chronograph-calculator watch. He will take over any conversation even when he knows nothing about the subject. He lives in the fast lane – he kisses the wives of wrestlers and holds the local hang-gliding record. He knows all the latest jokes and he tells them well. If he comes to a party then that party will be a success. His car is fire-engine red and it is the turbo model with the twin exhausts.

HE WILL LIKE ... Modern. Trendy

HE WILL DISLIKE ... dullness., conformit

The Spaniel

He has a high drive for FRIENDSHIP. Recognise him? He hates being alone – he is out every night or he has friends around to his place. He talks to complete strangers in lifts and queues. When he enters a room he goes around and introduces himself to everyone. He is embarrassingly generous and he will truly give you the shirt off his back. He has no personal secrets – he will tell you all the details of his operation or his last will and testament. He tries to please everybody and he smiles a lot. He hasn't an enemy in the world; how could he have? His car is a kombi – so he can take all his friends along.

HE WILL LIKE ... *if others do* ....

HE WILL DISLIKE ... *being diff* ....

The Owl

He has a high drive for MORALITY. Recognise him? He pays his debts 'to the penny' and he expects the same from you. You could trust him with a blank cheque or your pretty sister. He operates strictly according to the book; rules are everything. Last year a salesman gave him the usual bottle of the good stuff and he got thrown out of the Owl's office 'for trying to bribe me'. He thinks *Dallas* is the work of the devil; he is even worried about *The Wombles*. He is always scrupulously fair in everything he does, but there is not much mercy mixed into his justice. He is automatically elected to any committee and his opinion is respected. He has no sense of humour whatever. We don't know what sort of car he has but we are sure of one thing – it's paid for.

HE WILL LIKE ....

HE WILL DISLIKE ....

Before you look at my answers (which are not as important as yours; we look at these characters in a different light from each other because we are different human beings ourselves) we should recognise that the Customer Zoo is an over-simplification and the inhabitants are caricatures. People are not so easily put into categories; in fact, it is dangerous to file a man away by tagging him with an epithet. Nevertheless people do have different ways of looking at things, and if we can discern any sort of pattern in our prospect by watching and listening to him then we can adapt our approach so that we are walking on the same ground. This is the sort of thing which makes him tend to say: 'That man talks my language.'

[162]

Here are my answers; see if you agree. If you don't then you can have some fun deciding how little I know about my fellow man.

Squirrel: He will like anything which cossets his feeling for security, such as iron-clad guarantees about the product, testimonial letters attesting to the worth of the product, as much proof as you can give him that there is no risk in buying from the company. He will dislike any hint of high-pressure selling, any flash-in-the-pan company or fly-by-night salesman.

Lion: He will like anything which boosts his self-esteem; he demands deference from salesmen, an acknowledgement of his importance, a careful awareness of the fact that he is giving you some of his valuable time. One marvellous thing about the Lion is that he never worries overmuch about the price, just so long as what he is getting is recognised as the best. He orders by the truckload. He will hate any offhandedness; he will not touch the cheap and shoddy, he isn't impressed by a special bargain or a this-week-only discount and he is insulted if you offer it to him.

Dodo: He loves something which has been going, completely unchanged, for twenty years. Show him the tried and tested and he will buy. Anything which is traditional, solid, and mellowed by time is his thing. He will dislike the new, the untried, the innovative; don't show him light-emitting diodes or day-glo or quadrophonic or holographic. Don't wear your lilac silk suit, either; dress as if for a state funeral and you're in.

Peacock: He will like anything which the Dodo doesn't like, since he is almost the direct opposite of him. Show him the latest thing, the something which nobody has yet dreamed of; give him a new and dramatic way of doing something and he will bust a gut to have it at any cost. Anything about your product which will show him up in a bright light will do it. Let him do the talking – you needn't open your mouth, just nod from time to time. He will dislike anything plain, ordinary, purely functional, or lacking charisma or style.

Spaniel: He will like your product if he likes you; something of an exaggeration but a grain of truth there all the same. He responds well to the informal, first-name approach, and you will only embarrass him by insisting on his title when you talk to him. He will dislike, and be cast down by, any curtness, brusqueness or other display of cold formality. Remember that he may be the world's buddy, but he is not a fool, so break a promise to him and you are dead forever.

Owl: He will like the honest, down-to-earth, direct approach. He responds to the quiet and modest salesman who shows rather than talks too much. Stay on the subject and show a respect for his time (his company is paying him for it and he doesn't want to cheat the company). Be straight at all times with him and you will get straight dealing from him; his word will always be his bond. He will dislike the salesman who over-claims for his product, who swanks about his product or company or his own prowess. He doesn't like small-talk or socialising with salesmen – don't invite him out for a few snorts to celebrate the sale or there won't be a sale.

All right, your answers may have been different from mine but that's not important. This little exercise, while it might have seemed light-hearted and even frivolous, has an important base. As I have said many times, people are different. Find out in any way you can where my hot button is and you can sell to me; try to treat me the same way as you have treated the other seventeen people you have called on today and you will surely fail.

18

Let's get organised!

I might as well warn you that this chapter is the most boring one in the whole book. It is a bind to write and it will be a pain to read. There is nothing exciting or inspiring about organisation of a salesman's time and efforts. It's much more fun to be out there in the arena with the crowds cheering and the trumpets sounding than it is to be crouched over pieces of paper like a pen-pusher. Damn it, some of you entered the selling business to get away from pen-pushing!

Having said all that let me warn you also that you skip this chapter at your peril. You don't need to read it to be better at the art of selling; it has nothing to do with the selling process itself. But jump over it and go on to something more interesting and you could find yourself working harder to get less; you could wander off into the unknown and fail to understand why all this hard work isn't paying off as it should. I sometimes find the salesman who is over-organised; he spends so much of his time with charts, graphs, diagrams and lists that he never manages to get out and do any selling. I do find this person, yes, but very, very, seldom. Far more often do I come across the under-organised salesman, and it is for him that this chapter is written.

All right, let's get on with it since it is so vital to our success out in the field.

Tell you what; if you don't like the title at the top of this page (and I'm not crazy about it either) let's have a sub-title which describes the content just as well and is a lot easier to swallow. Here it is – how does it grab you?

THE LAZY SALESMAN'S PATH TO FAME AND FORTUNE

THE JOY OF SELLING

That's more like it, and it's true, too; the organised salesman is a lazy man – he can afford to be. To give just a few examples: he is so lazy that he thinks it makes sense to do something this evening which will take him thirty minutes, to save him two hours tomorrow; that's lazy. He is so lazy that before he climbs into a car and drives ten miles to see a man he does everything in his power to make sure that the man is there and ready to receive him – he's too lazy to make the trip twice. He is so lazy that in order to avoid calling back with a sample or brochure or whatever, he makes sure that on the *first* call he has all the samples or brochures or whatevers that he needs. He is lazy and he succeeds in what he attempts, without working up a sweat. I hope that you are lazy – if you are then you could be a success, too.

We shall be jumping around looking at various ways to go about the job of selling, using ways to do it well without doing it sweaty. Some of these will work for you, some not. Pick the ones you like and include them in your working philosophy.

First, I want to put into your hands one of the most useful pieces of paper that any salesman can have. It does one thing and one thing only, but it does it superbly well. Used properly, this piece of paper shows you where you are going strong in your selling efforts, and where you are going wrong – it shows you your strengths and your weaknesses. Now, wouldn't that be something that anyone would find useful? Let's try it out with some typical figures.

MONTHLY QUOTA: £60,000   TALKS-TO-SALES RATIO: 4:1

Calls	Sales Talks	Sales	Average Sale
200	120	30	£2,000

In order to set this up for yourself, first put down your monthly quota. The figure we have here is a money value amount, but of course it doesn't have to be; your quota could be in units sold, in gallons or cubic yards or tons – depends what you sell. For our example we have taken money, and this salesman has to sell £60,000 a month to keep everybody happy.

Then we introduce the concept of a ratio. Every salesman who ever lived has a ratio of the number of times he talks about his product to the man who can buy, compared with the number of times he makes a sale. This salesman's ratio is four to one, which means that in the next four hundred sales talks he will get around one hundred sales. You can of course work out your ratio by dividing a typical month's number of sales into the sales talks for that month.

Now divide the number of sales into your total sales for the past few months and this will give you the figure for the AVERAGE SALE column. Dividing this figure into your QUOTA will give you the NUMBER OF SALES column. In the case of our typical salesman, he has to make 30 sales each month – £2,000 into £60,000 – and from this figure of 30, and working on his ration of four to one, he gets the figure of 120 for the SALES TALKS column. For the NUMBER OF CALLS column he has to go to his records, or his knowledge and experience of his territory. Whatever the figure, it will of course be higher than the SALES TALKS column, because several of the CALLS he makes will not lead to SALES TALKS for one reason or another.

That's it; you are set up to make it work for you. If you have good records then to set this up will take, I suppose, one evening. Actually to run it every month? Not more than twenty minutes. Let's try some examples and see how it works. Our salesman keeps very close records and at the end of a month he finds a situation something like this:

	Calls	Sales Talks	Sales	Average Sale
Normal:	200	120	30	£2,000
Actual:	207	72	21	£1,978

We are ready to make this piece of paper work for us. First let us recognise that this salesman is in trouble; he does not have the number of sales which will give him his quota. Why? Where is he weak? Where has the balance between the columns broken down? Look carefully before you answer. Right – there is something wrong between CALLS and SALES TALKS. Note that he is working hard, all right; the number of CALLS is fine. It is just

[167]

that they are not leading to the right number of SALES TALKS. We don't know what this man sells or who he calls on, but his problem could be that he doesn't make appointments, that he is calling at the wrong time, or simply that he is talking to the wrong people. Whatever, it is clear where his trouble lies.

But take another look at that line of figures. We see that he is not making the right number of SALES TALKS, but what about those talks when he gets around to giving them? Are they good or bad? Of course they are good! 72 to 21 is very good indeed, since it is better than the ratio he has set himself. So we see a weakness in this man's operation, but there is also a strength. The whole point is that unless he did something like this exercise *there is no way that he would ever know*. He would only know that his sales figures were unsatisfactory and he would have no way to correct this state of affairs. I have had salesmen come to me in a panic, convinced that they had lost some magic in their sales presentations because their sales figures were going down like a pricked balloon. Together we have examined their situation and have found that there was nothing wrong with the talks at all; he simply was not giving enough of them.

One more example:

	Calls	Sales Talks	Sales	Average Sale
Normal:	200	120	30	£2,000
Actual:	137	94	24	£1,309

Again, he is in trouble, but what is the problem here? If you picked the CALLS column as the culprit you were right, but is it the number of calls, or the quality of those calls which is at fault? The number, of course; he isn't making enough of them. The quality of calling, you notice, is fine, since the ratio of 94 to 24 is perfectly satisfactory.

So all our man has to do is to increase the number of CALLS and everything will be fine? No, it isn't as easy as that, is it? There is ugly news under the AVERAGE SALE column. What could he be doing wrong? Well, perhaps if he turned back and read Coffee-break 3 on how to make some easy money he might be able to increase the figure. Perhaps he is simply grabbing the order, tucking it under his arm and running, perhaps he is working low-potential customers instead of going where the big bucks are – who knows? We can't know exactly *why* the figures are wrong without knowing more about his selling situation, but we certainly know *where* they are wrong.

Now, if you decide to use this idea, and I hope you do because it is custom-built for the lazy salesman, then don't worry too much about the exact headings which I have down here. The headings can be changed to suit your type of selling. To give you only one example of this let me put down the sort of thing which was worked out in a group of motorcar salesmen I was working with. They figured that none of my headings suited their sort of selling so this is what they ended up with:

PROSPECTS   TRADE-IN VALUATION   ROAD TEST   UNITS SOLD

They were not interested in the average sale because their quotas were based on number of units sold. See? The headings were all different, but the concept was the same – that you start with a certain effort and end with a certain result. All the way from the one to the other you are able to monitor where you are weak and where you are strong.

Paperwork

I suppose that if you didn't like the title 'Let's Get Organised' then you will hate the sub-title 'Paperwork'. I have yet to find a salesman who actually likes to fill in pieces of paper; I know I hate it, and I'm a salesman. Yet the lazy salesman does it because he knows that without a certain minimum of paperwork he is working too hard and not getting enough for his efforts.

If you are working in a half-way decent company then most of what I say here is not for you; you are already doing something like this. Most companies go further than I am doing here, because I am dealing with the absolute basic minimum of paperwork required in a salesman's day-to-day work. There are only three things you need to put on paper, but they represent the irreducible minimum, so you do need them all. You need to put down what you intend to do, what you have done, and what you know about your customers.

The first one, some sort of planning ahead, is easily done. I worked for years with nothing more than a page-a-day diary bought from a stationery store. Carry it with you and as you make appointments put them down immediately. You will probably be working a week or so ahead with this diary, and it is a simple matter to sit down on a Friday and look over the week to come and see where you are going to be on, say, next Wednesday. You see that you have an appointment in the northern part of your beat, so you look up other customers or prospects in that part and phone them for more appointments, filling Wednesday in very nicely. If your selling is not the sort where you make appointments then put down those people you will be seeing in that area. This way you can fill up your Wednesday to make it a worthwhile day.

Keep your planning diary with you at all times; not only are you able to record appointments as they come up but it is a constant reminder to you that you still have to call on people next week and next month. It forces you to think ahead.

The next piece of paperwork is a record of your calls. I know that a lot of salesmen don't do this, but take my word for it, it is absolutely vital. Before I did this I floundered around and wasted time which makes me shudder when I think back on it. Here you can also use a diary, and it can be the same sort exactly as the one you have for planning. The only difference is that the first one is being used a week ahead while the calls record is being filled in for this week – in fact, today.

Get into the habit of never starting the next call before you have written down the details of this one. Don't fall into the trap of believing that you can do all this at the end of the day because I promise you, you can't. You will forget that one little piece of information which you need to sell him on the next visit. Don't listen to salesmen who tell you that they have sold for years without this sort of record; maybe they have, but that doesn't prove that it is good practice. You won't believe the number of times you need to go back to your call record book and check up on something. Give you some examples to show what I mean:

Let's get organised!

You can find out how much time you are spending in each part of your territory, and tie this up with how much sales volume you are getting from each part. This could give you an entirely new idea of how to organise your calling pattern.

You can work out how many customers are giving you how much business in each section of your beat. This could change your call frequency pattern for different classes of buyers.

You can find out what *type* of business is giving you how much sales volume, and whether these are big, medium or small companies. You can only do this from call records, and you have to have it down on paper – you cannot work it out in your head.

There are other things that you can get from this sort of record but those examples should be enough to convince you that it really is worthwhile to keep those two diaries going. How long does it take? A minute or two for each call, and the rewards are big.

The third piece of paper is a record of what you know about your customer. Again, a lot of salesmen neglect this, but then a lot of people call two no-trumps with only twelve points, try to hit a three-wood out of heavy rough, and draw to an inside straight – that doesn't mean that it is smart.

Your company may have special paperwork for customer records. If not then do as I do – get a lot of six-by-eight cards and keep them in a simple 'tickler' file box. On these cards I put down *everything* I know about my client, no matter how trivial it may seem. I have a rule never to leave a client of mine without getting some piece of information to put on his card. The Personnel Manager has been transferred to the Consumer Division? Put it down. The Marketing Director has gone to visit some factories in Japan? Down it goes. I may never have reason to use that information, but – who knows? – I may. It is there if I want it.

Another thing; in my business of training, I don't have hundreds of regular companies as clients; I don't have more than about fifty. But as sure as nuts, every time I go through my client cards I find something which I have to do, something I promised a client – something! If someone broke in and stole my records I would be selling shoelaces on the corner by the end of the week – they are as important as that.

Check up on yourself

For this little exercise you will need a cheap notebook and a map of your territory. I say a cheap book because you will be using it for only one week after which you will flush it down the loo. You are going to check up on yourself.

Why should you want to do that? Well, the pro salesman is always looking for ways to increase his effectiveness, and the lazy salesman is trying to make sure that he isn't working too hard. Since you are both a pro salesman and a lazy person, we are going to combine these two ideologies – doing more while working less.

In the notebook on the first page put: MONDAY. Under that put 8.00 and leave four lines, then 9.00 and four more lines, right through to 5.00. That's your working day. Same thing for Tuesday through to Friday, and that's your week.

Now, the map of your territory. Don't bother to buy one, get one free from a service station or the tourist bureau. Depending on what your territory is, the map could be a piece of the countryside or it could be a street map of your town.

You are ready to go. Starting next Monday, put down *exactly* what you do in each hour of the day – leave *nothing* out. A typical hour could be; travelling, 15 minutes; seeing ABC company, 25 minutes; buying Mother's Day card, 10 minutes; telephoning for appointment, 5 minutes; filling in diary, 5 minutes.

At the same time, draw a line on your map of *exactly* where you went in that hour – everywhere! If you went five miles out of your way to buy theatre tickets then stick it in; don't cheat.

At the end of the week, sit down and go through the notebook and look at the map. You had better have a stiff drink next to you because if you are like the rest of us salesmen you will need it. Unless you are a most unusual person your hair will stand straight up in the air.

We waste a shocking amount of time, you know. Even the most

organised of us do. We back-track, we cross our tracks, we throw precious minutes and hours away as though we had an unlimited supply. We forget the angel who visits us every morning as we open our eyes and who deposits next to our beds our ration for the day. Count your ration tomorrow after the angel has left, and I'll bet you it is exactly the same as I got – just twenty-four hours, not a second more, not a second less. Sometimes I think that the difference between a successful salesman and a failure is nothing more than how the two go about using their ration.

That's it on organisation. We are all glad to be shot of it – except that the bad news is that you are not shot of it. If you are to be a successful salesman you never will be. Get organised and stay organised; life is so much easier that way!

COFFEE-BREAK 5: THERE ARE NO DULL PRODUCTS!

I was button-holed by a salesman after a talk I had given to a large group at a convention. He had a complaint to make about the content of my talk. He said: 'Mr Beer, you were talking in there about the excitement of selling and that may be all very well for the salesmen who sell exciting products; the lucky guys who handle sports cars and blue-chip stocks and high-fashion clothing and up-market computers and medical equipment have got it made. Look at me – who the hell can get excited about *rust-proofing*, for crying out loud?'

You may get to thinking about your products in this way at some time or another, so let's talk about it. You can't sell with excitement if you can't get excited about what you sell.

Here's a thought to hang on to in the dark days when your product range seems to lack the sparkle which it had when you first looked at it:

THERE ARE NO DULL PRODUCTS – THERE ARE ONLY DULL ATTITUDES TOWARDS PRODUCTS

I am thinking of four salesmen I know who are real cracker-jacks – they could sell Dean Martin on joining the Women's Christian Temperance Union. Here are their products; do they excite you?

- Paper for copying machines
- Householder's Insurance

- Razor blades
- Weedkilling equipment

You would go some distance before you found four products which on the face of it were less exciting than those. But do you know something? Those four salesmen must all be pretty stupid because *they all think they sell exciting products.*

Ask the copy paper salesman about his product and his eyes light up; he backs you into a corner and before you can get away you have heard the incredible story of the invention of the infrared copying process. Mention one word about his product to the insurance salesman and before you know it you are on a Chinese junk 600 years ago, where the idea of mutual insurance against shipwreck was first conceived. The razor blade salesman grows lyrical about the genius who first made stainless steel with a grain so fine that it was possible to put an edge on it. . . .

Maybe you get the idea, and I am sure that you are intelligent enough to realise that what we are talking about here is Michael Beer's old hobby horse – depth knowledge of your products. When you really know your product – its history, its development, its setbacks and its triumphs – that product suddenly becomes exciting.

There are no dull products. Rust-proofing? When you know all there is to know about it, man, that's an exciting product!

19

---

*Getting action
– piece of cake
or Mount Everest?*

I believe that all of us sales trainers in the world owe an apology to all salesmen in the world. I think that in one aspect of selling we have misled you very badly. We have written books on 'Closing the Sale'; we have produced films and tapes on 'Getting Action from the Customer'; we have spent thousands of hours in conference rooms discussing how to 'Get the Signature on the Order!'. In the process, we have built the closing of a sale into a frightening monster, an enormous step in the selling process.

And the truth is, it isn't like that at all.

You will see (I have seen many times, as I watched salesmen in the field) a salesman produce a perfectly competent sales presentation. He knows his product, he knows his customer's needs, he knows his opposition; he is in complete control of the interview. Then the time comes to wind the whole thing up, to get agreement and action from the listener, to close the sale. All at once this calm and confident salesman gulps, clears his throat, sneezes, blushes, and croaks out a request for the order.

Remember that this is the one part of the sales presentation where the customer knows exactly what you are doing. If the close worries the salesman as much as all this, what effect will it have on the customer? It will scare the life out of him, that's what it will do. The salesman looks desperate, and while you may feel sorry for desperate people you don't buy anything from them.

This salesman has been through sales training which has made the close of the sale into a Frankenstein monster. He has been loaded up with twenty-nine 'techniques' to help him get that order. This by itself is scary, because if you need all that ammunition to win then it must be like climbing Mount Everest stark naked and carrying a piano.

He has been brain-washed and conditioned into fearing this step, and how much of a chance does he have? I really don't know how this man ever gets an order with the way he feels about closing.

The truth about closing the sale is simply that its success does not depend on anything which we do at the end of the sales presentation at all; it depends on what we have done *during* that presentation.

Arnold Palmer has said that actually *hitting* the ball is the easiest part of the golf swing. This sounds fine, but he qualifies his statement by saying that before you hit the ball your grip, set-up and backswing must be done properly. In the same way, I believe that the close is the simplest part of the sales presentation. This sounds fine, too, but before we can get the order our customer knowledge, our fitting the product into his needs, the proof of our claims and the answering of all his questions must be properly done.

If all that *is* properly done the close is simple – a piece of cake. If all that is not properly done the close is almost impossible – Mount Everest.

I have heard a salesman explaining that he tried to close a prospect six separate times using six separate closing techniques. 'And would you believe, Michael, not one of them worked!' Oh, I believe it, Charlie, I do indeed. There was no way any of those techniques could have worked, because you didn't complete your backswing, your grip was wrong, you hadn't bothered to get your set-up right – you hadn't done the job properly up until then. You were trying to light a damp fire, start the car with a flat battery, write with an empty pen.

There is no easy road to closing. The full selling job must be done before we try for the order. If we fail to get that order it simply means that:

- We are talking to the wrong person.
- We haven't found his specific need.
- We haven't explained how the product fills this need.
- We haven't proved our claims.
- We haven't answered all his questions.

If we fail in one of these then no closing technique will help! If we succeed in all of them *then no closing technique is needed*! If you have been exposed to the sort of sales training which gives you a lot of closing techniques to learn by heart then you may find this difficult to believe, but it is true.

Hitting the ball or closing the sale is simple – but you have to get everything right before you even try.

20

So – what's holding you back?

That's it.

That is all I am going to put on paper about the wonderful world of selling. It isn't all I could write – I could fill another complete book with examples and stories of salesmen at work, but this is all you need if you decide to go ahead and join the happy breed of people who make their living by going out and selling things to other people.

Although I wrote Part One as though you had not yet got into selling and Part Two as though you were already in, I am sure that you have read the whole book through before making the big decision: Do I or don't I?

So – what's holding you back? One or two points which might help you to make up your mind:

The 'I would look a fool' worry

How many people would be leading different lives if it were not for this thought?

The terror of making a fool of oneself has kept countless thousands of people from striking out and taking a new path. They fear the derision and contempt of their peers and this keeps them on the conventional, 'safe' road of the non-success. On this road at least no-one can point a finger and say: 'Well, what did he expect? He was bound to make a fool of himself!'

We have all had this fear to a greater or lesser degree, manifested in some way or another:

- 'People will think I'm crazy.'
- 'None of my friends has ever done anything like this.'
- 'I'll get a lot of uphill from my family if I do it.'
- 'Our class of people doesn't do that sort of thing.'

And so on. We fear the unconventional, the off-beat, the way-out and when we lose in the same way that others around us are losing, that somehow makes it acceptable.

An immigrant from one of the Mitteleuropa countries turned up on our shores some years ago without a word of English to his name and with just enough money in his pocket to buy one roll of cloth. He got someone to write on a piece of card the legend '9/6d per yard!' He want from door to door, holding up the cloth and displaying his written sales talk. People laughed; he laughed with them. He sold the roll, bought himself some bread and cheese and another roll of cloth and off he went again. Lots of people got a lot of laughs out of this nutcase with his roll of cloth and his grubby card. Now, as people pass this man's textile factory you don't hear much laughing. He was not afraid of making a fool of himself.

A friend of mine left school at the same time that I did and became a carpenter's apprentice. Our school was not the sort of place which produced *tradesmen*. From there you were expected to go to university or enter some sort of business; we were white-collar, middle-class people, not blue-collar peasants. This crazy character almost drowned in the funny remarks from his classmates when he made it known that he was going to spend the rest of his life sawing wood and knocking in nails. I don't imagine that there are many funny remarks these days as his signs go up all over the place with his name and the title 'Master Builder'.

We had our share of losers in that class, same as any other group of people. I wonder what they think when they see what has happened to the stupid carpenter's apprentice.

Neither of these examples happens to be directly concerned with selling as a career, but that is not the point; the point is that whether you decide to become a salesman or not is up to you – but don't let the 'I would look a fool' worry keep you from taking the step.

So – what's holding you back?

The 'What if I fail?' nightmare

I get phone calls from people who have read something I have written in a book or an article about selling. In several things I have written I have made the point that selling is one of the quickest ways of making money without qualifications, long apprenticeships of any special aptitude or skill.

These calls usually start off by asking whether a crash course will turn the caller into a successful salesman. When I have to tell him it will not, he asks whether it would be difficult for him to sell, seeing that he has had no selling experience. I say: 'Look, selling isn't easy, but if you really and truly *want* to sell then yes, you will be able to.'

A pause always follows. Then: 'Are you sure?' I say: 'Yes, I'm sure. All you have to do is want it so badly that you force yourself to do the things which will make you a good salesman. Then you will succeed. I promise you.' Another pause. 'Well, thank you for talking to me, Mr Beer,' and he rings off.

I have had this conversation many times and it always depresses me. These people must want to change from what they are doing. There must be dissatisfaction with their present situation. By picking up the telephone they are making the first faltering step towards change; dammit, there is *motivation* there! But I can tell from the hopeless way that they say: 'Well, thank you for talking to me,' that another door has closed for them. The fear of failure has them locked in its icy grip – helpless, immobile.

I feel guilty after these conversations. I feel I should say: 'Wait! Don't hang up. It's true that I can't help you become what you want – only you can do that. But don't pull out of the race even before the gun goes off. Have faith in yourself. Don't let the fear of failure cripple you before you even try to walk.'

I don't say this because I try to stay out of other people's destinies, which is a sneaky way of saying that I am like the Levite and the Priest, remember? I don't say it but I do feel tempted to. That man will go back to doing the job which he dislikes so much that he had to phone me. He will tell his wife that he has spoken to me but that the chasm is too wide to leap, the rapids too treacherous to shoot, the risk of failure too great.

[181]

The Kamikaze compulsion

On the other side of the scale from the 'What if I fail' nightmare is the Kamikaze compulsion. Occasionally a man will leap into the unknown with no thought for the result, no idea of what he is doing, no knowledge of where he is going or how to get there. When he fails in this madness – as he richly deserves to – his excuse is: 'Well, at least I tried!' Perhaps, but you don't sink every penny into an indelible pencil factory when the ball-point has killed the indelible pencil stone dead. That isn't the glorious and courageous endeavour that its perpetrator would like us to think, that is a death-wish.

Don't let anything in this book give you the idea that you can set off across the ocean without a map, compass, or rudder and expect that the gods will admire your foolhardiness and some-how lead you to a golden shore. If you really want to change – and I hope you will, rather than sitting around regretting for the rest of your life that you didn't – for the love of heaven don't submit to the Kamikaze compulsion and rush into the first selling job you can get.

When you do decide to go for it, it is not negative thinking to ask yourself: 'What is the very worst that could happen?' Last month I was talking to a man who has succeeded in getting the agency for a product from Taiwan. He is excited about the idea and from the way he described it to me the potential does seem good. But this man is no fool; before he committed himself, before he signed a single piece of paper, he worked out the very worst things that could possibly happen. This may sound as if he was suffering from the 'What if I fail?' nightmare, but this isn't so. Looking realistically at what can happen has not stopped him from going ahead; it has merely helped him to recognise the possible pitfalls. He realises very well that this is the biggest thing he has ever done in business, and he is determined to get it right.

You are probably thinking of joining a company and selling its products rather than being your own boss as this man was con-sidering. However, it may help to clear things in your own mind if you see how he trod the fine line between, on the one hand, jumping in where angels feared to tread, and on the other, being afraid to move at all. Here is his list of what he called the Awful Possibilities, with his comments on each in brackets:

So – what's holding you back?

1. I may not be able to get the loan from the bank in order to start. (Unlikely; preliminary talks with the bank officials have been encouraging. If I don't get it I lose nothing because my contract is contingent on getting the loan.)

2. My Far East principals may stop production of the product. (Most unlikely; the product is doing well.)

3. A better product may appear on the market. (Possible. However, I shall be the first in the field with this product in this country. When I have established it I shall diversify to dilute the risk of competition beating me.)

4. A cheaper product may appear on the market. (Possible. However, mine will be better, and there will always be a market for the high-quality product; I will keep a good share of the market. I intend to watch the market carefully from the price angle.)

5. Some hi-jacker may talk my principals into switching the agency to him. (Not possible. The contract will tie them up tight.)

6. A severe recession may hit the country, and my product is a luxury, not a necessity. (Most unlikely, but anything is possible. In this case I should be stuck with only one shipment of product, since I shall order the next only when the first is almost completely sold. This won't break me, and in any case a recession will mean only that sales will slow down, not stop altogether.)

7. I have had one heart attack, and my health may fail so that I can no longer carry on. (Interesting work won't kill you; sitting around worrying about your health just might. Forget it.)

That's it. Those are the Awful Possibilities for this man – all of them. What would you do in his position? You would go for it. You would not be intimidated by the 'What if I fail?' nightmare, but you would have avoided the Kamikaze compulsion. Confident that whatever happened you would be able to handle it, you would go ahead.

When preparing for an important sales presentation the pro salesman often asks himself: 'What is the strongest objection they can possibly throw at me?' *This is not negative thinking.* The salesman asks himself this so that he can plan his strategy to encompass this Awful Possibility. He knows then that if it does eventuate it will not catch him flat-footed; he will be ready to give it the best counter. This gives him tremendous confidence – and when, as so often happens, the Awful Possibility does not occur, his confidence is strengthened even further.

Only you can decide your personal destiny. In the matter of what you are going to do with the rest of your life, only you can walk the last mile – you walk it alone. You can read books, talk it over with good friends and listen to wise counsellors, but in the end the decision is yours. It may help to turn back to the quotation by H. G. Wells in the front of this book and read it again; it once helped me to make a decision which affected my whole life.

If you do decide to enter the wonderful world of selling, remember that you *will* succeed, you can't help succeeding, if you are ready to meet the two conditions: you have to *want* it, and you have to come into it with no reservations, no hesitation, and hit it with everything you've got.

Welcome!

INDEX

Index